Prefect Workflow Orchestration Essentials

Definitive Reference for Developers and Engineers

Richard Johnson

Contents

Introduction

Workflow orchestration has become a foundational element in the field of data engineering and computational pipeline management. As data complexity and scale have grown dramatically, the ability to design, execute, monitor, and maintain intricate workflows reliably and efficiently has emerged as a critical organizational capability. This book presents a comprehensive treatment of Prefect, a contemporary workflow orchestration platform that addresses many of the challenges inherent to modern pipeline orchestration.

Prefect distinguishes itself through a flexible architecture and intuitive programming model that supports declarative and dynamic workflow construction. Its design accommodates diverse operational environments, from local development systems to large-scale distributed infrastructures, enabling seamless scalability and adaptability. Prefect's modular components and deployment options provide a robust foundation for building resilient pipelines with precise control over execution semantics and failure handling.

This volume begins by establishing a solid understanding of workflow orchestration principles and the architectural underpinnings of Prefect. We examine Prefect in relation to other orchestration tools such as Airflow, Luigi, and Dagster, highlighting comparative strengths and design philosophies. Key abstractions like flows, tasks, and states are dissected to illuminate how workflow logic is modeled and managed, along with Prefect's flexible deployment strategies and security considerations.

Moving into practical usage, the book provides an in-depth exploration of Prefect Core programming constructs. Readers will gain proficiency in defining complex workflows programmatically, managing state transitions, implementing advanced control flow mechanisms, and applying sophisticated error recovery tactics. Attention is given to performance optimization through caching, results handling, and rigorous workflow testing to ensure reliability in production environments.

A detailed examination of Prefect's execution engine reveals how workflows are scheduled, serialized, and executed across various computational contexts, including local, parallel, and distributed settings. Prefect's agent infrastructure and event-driven design are discussed to demonstrate dynamic resource management and responsiveness. Observability features such as logging, monitoring, and instrumentation are presented as essential tools for operational excellence.

The book further addresses the critical topics of workflow reliability, scalability, and performance tuning. Strategies for fault tolerance, disaster recovery, and throughput enhancement are laid out to guide readers in building robust orchestration solutions that meet demanding service-level objectives. Methods for accommodating non-deterministic tasks and managing execution complexity are also covered.

Integration with external systems and ecosystems is a major focus, recognizing the interconnected nature of modern data platforms. Prefect's capabilities for interfacing with databases, cloud storage, APIs, message queues, and DevOps toolchains are thoroughly explained. Special consideration is given to security practices around secrets management, authentication, and compliance to align workflow operations with organizational governance requirements.

Advanced usage scenarios explore customization through task libraries, dynamic workflows, scheduling, and extensibility via plugins and APIs. Visualization and user interface tools are discussed to enhance the interpretability and management of workflows at scale. Security and governance topics ensure readers understand how to maintain compliance, protect data privacy, and implement audit mechanisms.

Operational excellence is emphasized through topics such as monitoring, alerting, cost management, incident response, documentation, and continuous improvement. Real-world case studies highlight best practices and lessons learned from managing large-scale flows, providing practical insights that complement the theoretical foundation.

Finally, the book looks forward to emerging trends in orchestration, including serverless computing, AI-driven workflow management, cross-platform orchestration, and evolving community standards. This forward-looking perspective equips practitioners with the context to anticipate and adapt to the future landscape of workflow orchestration.

Through detailed explanations, practical examples, and expert guidance, this book aims to empower data engineers, DevOps professionals, and developers to leverage Prefect effectively. Readers will gain a comprehensive understanding of how to design, implement, and maintain complex workflows that drive operational efficiency and innovation within their organizations.

Chapter 1

Foundations of Workflow Orchestration

Dive into the world of modern data and computation with a behind-the-scenes look at workflow orchestration—an essential discipline powering today's complex, scalable pipelines. This chapter unpacks the 'why' and 'how' of orchestrating tasks at scale, explores critical architecture choices, and sets the stage for understanding both the power and subtleties of Prefect's orchestration model.

1.1. The Role of Workflow Orchestration in Modern Data Engineering

The exponential growth of data volume and complexity, driven by advances in sensor networks, social media, IoT devices, and enterprise systems, has transformed the landscape of data engineering. This transformation is fundamentally intertwined with the evolution of workflow orchestration, which has become an indispensable discipline within modern data engineering frameworks. Workflow orchestration refers to the automated arrangement, coordination, and management of complex computational processes-principally data pipelines-that must execute in a robust, timely, and fault-tolerant manner across diverse and often distributed computing environments.

At its core, the rise of big data and cloud computing precipitated a departure from monolithic, manually coordinated data processing scripts toward modular, scalable pipelines that integrate heterogeneous data sources and computational frameworks. Traditional batch processing workflows, often developed as isolated or loosely coordinated tasks, fail to meet the agility and reliability demands imposed by contemporary analytical use cases. Workflow orchestration platforms emerged to fill this gap by providing a unified control plane for sequencing, scheduling, and monitoring interdependent processing stages, as well as enforcing data and task dependencies.

Historically, the earliest orchestration solutions were rudimentary job schedulers limited to linear or simple task execution patterns. As data pipelines grew in complexity-incorporating extract-transform-load (ETL) operations, machine learning model training, and real-time streaming ingestion-so did the complexity of dependency graphs. Modern orchestration systems introduce directed acyclic graph (DAG) abstractions to represent these dependencies explicitly, enabling precise execution order control and conditional branching. This abstraction safeguards data consistency and integrity, ensuring that downstream computations commence only once all prerequisite tasks are complete.

Moreover, cloud environments have rendered static resource allocation insufficient, necessitating elastic and dynamic execution models. Orchestration platforms now integrate natively with cloud-native technologies such as container orchestration (e.g., Kubernetes) and serverless functions, enabling scalable resource provisioning aligned with pipeline demand. This capability is critical in scenarios where workloads fluctuate widely by time of day or data arrival patterns, promoting cost efficiency without compromising throughput or latency.

Data engineers and data scientists both benefit substantially from workflow orchestration. For engineers, orchestration abstracts away the choreography of diverse services, languages, and runtime environments, reducing operational overhead and accelerating development cycles. For data scientists, orchestration automates repetitive training and evaluation processes, enabling rapid iteration and deployment of machine learning models. Importantly, workflow orchestration platforms support parameterization, enabling pipelines to adapt dynamically to varying input schemas, data volumes, or experimental settings, which is vital in research and production environments alike.

Reliability constitutes a central challenge addressed by orchestration. Data pipelines often involve brittle components susceptible to transient failures such as network glitches, service outages, or data corruption. Orchestration systems embed sophisticated error handling strategies, including automatic retries, alerting mechanisms, and checkpointing, to minimize disruption. Fine-grained monitoring and logging enable prompt identification and diagnosis of failure modes, thus reducing mean time to recovery (MTTR) and improving pipeline availability.

Scheduling is another crucial facet intricately managed by orchestration platforms. Pipelines operating at massive scale frequently process continuous data streams or adhere to strict batch windows. Scheduling logic must accommodate diverse triggering mechanisms: time-based (cron-like), event-driven (arrival of new files or messages), and manual invocation. Advanced orchestration frameworks provide flexible policy configurations to define priori-

7

ties, concurrency limits, and resource quotas, ensuring adherence to service-level agreements (SLAs) without resource contention.

Managing complex dependencies across distributed systems raises additional consistency concerns. Distributed coordination must guarantee that tasks sharing external state or writing to common storage do so in a manner that prevents race conditions or deadlocks. Modern orchestration frameworks often incorporate transactional semantics or integrate with distributed coordination services (e.g., Apache ZooKeeper, etcd) to ensure atomic state transitions and consistency guarantees.

Workflow orchestration has evolved to address the unique and expanded needs dictated by big data and cloud computing paradigms. By abstracting and automating the management of dependencies, scheduling, and resilience, orchestration platforms empower data engineers and scientists to build scalable, robust, and adaptive data pipelines. This functionality is critical not only for maintaining operational continuity but also for fostering innovation through iterative experimentation and rapid deployment processes intrinsic to data-driven decision-making.

1.2. Overview of Prefect: Architecture and Ecosystem

Prefect is a modern workflow orchestration tool designed to address challenges inherent in managing complex data pipelines and automations within dynamic cloud-native environments. Emerging in response to limitations seen in traditional schedulers and orchestration platforms, Prefect emphasizes reliability, modularity, and observability as foundational principles. Its architecture and ecosystem reflect a nuanced design philosophy aimed at seamlessly integrating with contemporary data stacks while providing a scalable and extensible framework.

At its core, Prefect operates around the concept of declarative work-flow definitions, referred to as *Flows*, which are composed of dis-crete *Tasks*. This abstraction allows users to define dependen-cies explicitly and express complex execution graphs programmat-ically, using Python as the lingua franca. Prefect's flows are inher-ently modular, enabling reuse and composability, which align well with modern software engineering practices.

The architectural design of Prefect bifurcates responsibilities be-tween the *Core* and the *Orchestration Layer*, efficiently separating workflow authoring from execution control and monitoring. Pre-fect Core is the open-source foundation that users interact with when building flows and tasks. It manages execution logic, retries, caching, and state management on the local or remote agents. This modular boundary allows Prefect Core to be fully agnostic of under-lying infrastructure while supporting pluggable execution targets such as Kubernetes clusters, cloud virtual machines, or serverless environments.

The Orchestration Layer-served primarily by Prefect Cloud (a managed SaaS offering) or Prefect Server (self-hosted)-provides centralized state tracking, scheduling, and an observability interface. This layer functions as a control plane, coordinating the distributed execution of tasks while maintaining metadata on flow runs, logs, failure alerts, and performance metrics. Such telemetry offers crucial insights into operational health, facilitating root cause analysis and performance optimizations. The orchestration backend is built using modern technologies optimized for scalability and low-latency state propagation, commonly leveraging RESTful APIs and message queues for communication between agents and the server.

Prefect's architecture also includes *Agents*, lightweight processes that poll the orchestration service for work and execute task runs in designated compute environments. Agents serve as adapters be-tween Prefect's control plane and heterogeneous execution targets.

The extensibility of agent implementations permits deployment on local machines, cloud providers, container orchestrators, or hybrid environments. This abstraction simplifies operational complexity and enables seamless scaling of workflow executions.

Prefect's design philosophy is fundamentally pragmatic, striving to empower users with a rich yet unobtrusive interface that encourages best practices without enforcing rigid conventions. It deliberately avoids imposing heavyweight domain-specific languages or monolithic runtimes, favoring Python's readability and rich ecosystem. The framework embraces failure as a first-class citizen; tasks emit explicit state changes that orchestrators and downstream dependencies can react to, enabling dynamic error handling, branching, and state transitions.

Historically, Prefect arose from the growing need for flexible orchestration beyond what platforms like Apache Airflow offered. While Airflow pioneered many workflow scheduling concepts, its limitations in dynamic pipeline definition, real-time observability, and cloud-native integration motivated Prefect's creation. Prefect thus represents a new generation of orchestration tools designed explicitly for the scale, velocity, and diversity of modern data ecosystems.

Within the broader landscape, Prefect complements components such as data processing frameworks (e.g., Apache Spark, Dask), cloud infrastructure providers (AWS, GCP, Azure), and storage solutions. It integrates seamlessly with containerization and orchestration technologies such as Docker and Kubernetes, enhancing portability and resilience. Furthermore, Prefect's pluggable architecture supports broad integration with data ingestion, transformation, and analytics tools, enabling end-to-end managed pipelines.

Prefect's ecosystem extends beyond the core orchestration platform, encompassing a rich plugin system and community-driven integrations. Connectors for various cloud services, database systems, messaging platforms, and monitoring tools provide extensibility critical for enterprise-grade deployments. Additionally, the Prefect API enables automation and customization of workflow lifecycles, while its UI and CLI tools offer user-friendly interfaces for deployment, monitoring, and debugging.

Prefect's architecture embodies a modular, scalable, and resilient approach to workflow orchestration, blending declarative task management with imperative execution control. Its ecosystem reflects a flexible and integrative stance, allowing seamless adoption into modern cloud and data infrastructures without sacrificing observability or control. This positioning grants Prefect both robustness and agility, making it a compelling choice for organizations aiming to operationalize complex, scalable data workflows in heterogeneous environments.

1.3. Comparison of Orchestration Tools: Prefect vs. Airflow, Luigi, and Dagster

The landscape of workflow orchestration tools is dominated by several well-established frameworks, each distinguished by specific architectural paradigms, feature sets, and operational philosophies. Prefect, Airflow, Luigi, and Dagster collectively represent the cornerstone of current orchestration technology, yet their suitability varies considerably depending on the use case and infrastructure requirements. A granular comparison reveals the nuances guiding the selection of these tools based on reliability, scalability, extensibility, and usability.

Airflow employs a Directed Acyclic Graph (DAG)-based abstraction for workflow definition, emphasizing task dependencies and scheduling via static Python scripts enriched with a declarative API. This model excels for batch pipelines with periodic scheduling, supporting dynamic generation of DAGs but within a largely static construct. Luigi shares Airflow's DAG-oriented approach but predates it and leans towards simplicity, eschewing the complexity of a scheduler webserver and focusing on pipeline definitions with dependency resolution through a centralized scheduler.

Prefect advances this paradigm by introducing a hybrid control flow model that separates task execution logic from orchestration concerns. It leverages the concept of "flows" defined imperatively in Python with dynamic and conditional branching capabilities supported inherently. Prefect's orchestration layer operates either in a cloud-managed environment (Prefect Cloud) or via Prefect Server, facilitating greater flexibility and orchestration metadata management, including richer state handling and retries.

Dagster's distinctive contribution lies in its strong emphasis on data-aware orchestration, integrating type systems and asset materializations directly in pipeline definitions. The framework promotes modularity with composable solids (tasks) and emphasizes observability and introspection through its type system and metadata capture. Workflow execution is managed by a daemon process with rich event logging and built-in testing support.

Scheduling and Execution: Airflow, with its mature scheduler and executor plugins (including Celery and Kubernetes Executors), offers robust options for scaling workflows horizontally across clusters. Its time-based scheduling is highly configurable, but static DAGs limit the dynamic adaptation of workflows at runtime. Luigi, while simpler, provides imperative task definitions with strong dependency tracking but lacks sophisticated scheduler and UI capabilities for large-scale deployments.

Prefect's flexible scheduling integrates seamlessly with external schedulers or Prefect Cloud's managed scheduler. Its dynamic flow definitions allow event-driven and condition-based workflow paths, accommodating real-time decision logic that static DAGs struggle with. Dagster incorporates cron-like scheduling but places more importance on triggering pipelines based on upstream data changes or asset materialization rather than purely time-based schedules.

State Management and Failure Handling: Prefect's unique state machine architecture enables advanced state transitions with context propagation, enabling automated retries, failure notifications, and granular task-level monitoring. Airflow supports retries and SLA misses with a conventional task instance state model, though it requires additional setups like sensors or custom callbacks for complex error handling.

Dagster offers a sophisticated asset lineage tracking model, providing visibility into data dependencies and pipeline health, which enables precise failure isolation. Luigi's failure handling is more rudimentary, primarily involving task retries and re-execution of failed tasks without native lineage or sophisticated state tracking.

Extensibility and Integration: Airflow boasts an extensive ecosystem and plugin architecture, enabling integration with a wide variety of data sources, cloud services, and third-party tools. Its REST API and web UI provide comprehensive operational control. Conversely, Luigi is comparatively limited, frequently necessitating custom development for non-trivial integrations.

Prefect emphasizes a modern, RESTful API-first design, facilitating seamless integration with Kubernetes, Docker, and major cloud providers. It supports user-defined task libraries and a pluggable executor model, enabling orchestration customization suited to microservice architectures and CI/CD pipelines. Dagster's type system and metadata allow for sophisticated pipeline composition and validation, promoting rigorous testing and deployment workflows integrated with version control and CI.

User Experience and Observability: Airflow's web interface is mature and widely adopted but can be cumbersome when managing highly dynamic or non-linear workflows. Prefect's UI delivers live flow visualization with real-time logs and state summaries, designed for both developers and data engineers requiring rapid debugging and iteration. Dagster's UI uniquely focuses on data asset perspectives, pipeline lineage, and type-aware introspection, enabling deeper understanding of data transformations and dependencies.

Luigi provides a minimalist web interface and CLI, focusing on straightforward pipeline management without advanced visualization or monitoring features.

Prefect's strength lies in its modern, Python-native API, flexible execution model, and cloud-native orchestration capabilities which excel in complex, conditional workflows and real-time dynamic pipelines. Its emphasis on state management and observability caters to production-grade reliability. However, dependence on Prefect Cloud for full enterprise features may introduce vendor lock-in considerations.

Airflow remains the de facto standard for large batch ETL workflows with extensive ecosystem support and robust scheduling. Its limitations arise in handling dynamic workflows, intricate conditional logic, or real-time event-driven pipelines without significant extensions.

Luigi offers simplicity and ease of use for straightforward batch pipelines but lacks scalability and enterprise features such as a rich scheduler, UI, and integrations compared to contemporary tools.

Dagster is ideal for data-centric orchestration requiring strong type-safety, asset tracking, and end-to-end visibility. Its design imposes a steeper learning curve and may be overkill for simpler pipeline orchestration needs.

Key factors influencing the choice among these frameworks include:

- **Workflow Complexity:** Dynamic, event-driven, or branching workflows favor Prefect or Dagster; static, schedule-driven workflows suit Airflow or Luigi.

- **Data Lineage and Observability Requirements:** DAG-level monitoring and asset tracking capabilities in Dagster excel where data provenance is critical.

- **Operational Scale and Ecosystem:** Airflow's mature ecosystem is advantageous for organizations seeking extensive third-party integrations and cluster scaling.

- **Developer Productivity and Extensibility:** Prefect's Python-native, imperative API enhances rapid development and adaptability.

- **Deployment Model and Vendor Dependency:** Luigi and Airflow offer open-source, on-premises deployments, whereas Prefect and Dagster increasingly rely on cloud or hybrid architectures.

Thus, aligning the orchestration tool's paradigms with organizational pipeline complexity, integration demands, and operational constraints ensures optimal workflow automation and maintainability.

1.4. Conceptual Model: Flows, Tasks, and States

At the core of Prefect's orchestration framework lie three fundamental abstractions—*Flows*, *Tasks*, and *States*—which together provide a robust model for designing and managing complex computation and data pipelines. Understanding how these elements interact is essential to leveraging Prefect's capabilities for creating reliable, observable, and maintainable workflows.

Flows: The Structure of Orchestration

A *Flow* constitutes the overarching logical structure that defines the sequence and dependencies of execution units in a data or computation pipeline. Conceptually, it can be likened to a directed acyclic graph (DAG), where each node represents a discrete computational step, and the edges dictate the execution order. Prefect Flows serve as containers that organize and encapsulate multiple Tasks, governing how data and control signals propagate throughout the pipeline.

Flows are dynamic entities that not only define static graph structures but also facilitate runtime modifications such as conditional branching, loops, and parameter passing. Through concise Python-based constructs, the user expresses complex control flows, integrating error handling and retries as inherent workflow properties. This abstraction allows the pipeline to be modular, reusable, and easily testable.

Tasks: The Fundamental Execution Units

Within a Flow, *Tasks* represent the atomic units of work—individual computations, data transformations, API calls, or any discrete operation required by the pipeline. Each Task encapsulates a well-defined piece of business logic or data processing, designed to be idempotent and side-effect aware to enhance reliability. A task is implemented as a Python callable, often decorated or wrapped by Prefect's Task API extensions to enable execution tracking and lifecycle management.

Tasks are not isolated; they express dependencies through input and output relationships, enabling Prefect to construct an execution plan that respects data lineage and inter-task sequencing. The flexibility of defining custom tasks or composing built-in primitives allows developers to model arbitrary complexities without sacrificing readability or control.

States: Tracking Execution and Outcomes

Prefect's *State* abstraction embodies the lifecycle status of a Task or Flow at runtime. States transition through well-defined stages such as Pending, Running, Success, Failed, and Skipped, with additional intermediate or custom states representing retries, pauses, or cancellations. This state machinery is pivotal for monitoring, fault tolerance, and conditional logic within workflows.

The State system transforms the execution model from a simple fire-and-forget operation into a controllable, introspectable process. For example, when a Task fails, its State changes accordingly, triggering retry policies or error handlers defined at the Flow level. These State transitions also serve as rich event data for Prefect's UI and logging infrastructure, enabling detailed observability and audit trails necessary for production-grade pipeline management.

Interactions Among Flows, Tasks, and States

The interplay between Flows, Tasks, and States manifests in a comprehensive and adaptive orchestration mechanism. Consider a Flow representing an ETL pipeline: multiple Tasks perform extraction, cleaning, transformation, and loading steps, each responsible for propagating their output downstream. During execution, Prefect monitors the State of each Task—only advancing when predecessor Tasks reach terminal success states, or invoking fallback logic if failures occur.

This relationship is illustrated by the monitoring of Task output dependencies: a Task enters the Running State only after all its upstream dependencies are in the Success State, ensuring correct sequencing and data availability. If a Task encounters an error and transitions to Failed, the Flow's error handling policies inspect these States and decide whether to retry the Task, skip subsequent dependent Tasks, or abort the entire Flow.

Practical Analogy and Example

To ground these abstractions, imagine orchestrating a multi-step document processing pipeline analogous to an assembly line in a factory. The Flow represents the entire production line blueprint. Each Task corresponds to a station on the line performing a specific operation: OCR scanning, language translation, text summarization, and final storage. The States act as operational flags for

17

each station—whether it is ready to begin, actively processing, has completed successfully, or needs human intervention due to an error.

Implementing this in Prefect might involve defining the Flow and Tasks as follows:

```
from prefect import Flow, task

@task
def ocr_scan(document):
    # extract text from scanned document
    return extracted_text

@task
def translate(text, target_lang):
    # translate extracted text
    return translated_text

@task
def summarize(text):
    # generate summary from the text
    return summary

@task
def store_result(summary):
    # save summary to database
    pass

with Flow("Document Processing Pipeline") as flow:
    doc = "input_document.pdf"
    extracted_text = ocr_scan(doc)
    translated_text = translate(extracted_text, target_lang="en")
    summary = summarize(translated_text)
    store_result(summary)
```

During execution, Prefect manages the States of each Task, ensuring, for instance, that the translate Task only starts after the ocr_scan Task successfully completes. If ocr_scan fails, its State transitions appropriately, and the Flow may halt or activate retry logic depending on predefined policies.

Extensibility and Advanced Control

Beyond sequencing, Prefect's Task and State model supports advanced features such as dynamic mapping (parallel task invocations over collections), conditional branching based on State or output, and custom State handlers to integrate with external monitoring or notification systems. This extensible framework empowers developers to build intricate, reactive pipelines that respond intelligently to both data conditions and runtime anomalies.

The conceptual model of Flows, Tasks, and States provides a unified language for expressing data pipelines as modular, interactive, and resilient systems. By abstracting orchestration mechanics behind these core abstractions, Prefect enables developers to focus on the logic of computation and data movement rather than the complexities of execution control, error handling, and state persistence.

1.5. Prefect Deployment Models: Cloud, Server, and Hybrid

Prefect offers a flexible array of deployment models that cater to diverse organizational requirements for workflow orchestration. These deployment options—Prefect Cloud, Prefect Server, and hybrid configurations—differ significantly in terms of infrastructure control, operational complexity, scalability, and cost. An in-depth analysis of these models reveals the trade-offs and considerations that guide the optimal choice for a given environment.

Prefect Cloud is a fully managed, SaaS-based solution that abstracts away the complexity of orchestration infrastructure. By offloading infrastructure management to the Prefect team, users gain rapid access to a robust, scalable platform without the need for dedicated DevOps resources. The architecture encompasses reusable API endpoints, a centralized metadata database, a UI server, and agents that interact with user-defined flows. Key advantages include out-of-the-box alerting, logging, security updates, and high availability, backed by the cloud provider's SLAs. Prefect Cloud integrates seamlessly with popular authentication providers

19

via OAuth and offers secure storage of credentials and secrets through its Vault integration. However, this convenience incurs ongoing subscription costs and potential limitations on customization or data residency due to multi-tenancy.

In contrast, Prefect Server presents an open-source, self-hosted alternative for organizations requiring greater control over their orchestration stack. Prefect Server consists of a collection of microservices and a PostgreSQL database, all orchestrated through Kubernetes or equivalent container orchestration platforms. Deploying Prefect Server demands skilled infrastructure engineering, with responsibilities including cluster maintenance, security hardening, backup strategies, and monitoring. This approach enables complete data ownership and customization of the orchestration environment, essential for compliance-driven sectors or environments with strict data sovereignty requirements. Scaling Prefect Server hinges on the underlying Kubernetes cluster's capacity and configured resource limits. The maintenance overhead, while nontrivial, can be mitigated by automated CI/CD pipelines and Infrastructure as Code (IaC) techniques, but it remains a critical operational consideration.

Bridging these extremes is the hybrid deployment model, which utilizes cloud-managed components alongside self-hosted infrastructure. Typically, this pattern involves running agents and flow execution workloads on-premises or within private clouds, connected to Prefect Cloud's orchestration backend. This arrangement leverages cloud-hosted orchestration benefits while maintaining execution close to sensitive datasets or specialized computing resources, such as GPUs or proprietary clusters. Hybrid deployment can reduce latency, enhance security controls, and comply with regulatory frameworks by minimizing data egress. Key challenges include network configuration, firewall management, and ensuring reliable connectivity between self-hosted agents and the cloud API endpoints. Additionally, hybrid architectures often require careful configuration of authentication tokens, secure tunnels (e.g., VPN or SSH), and potentially custom logging pipelines to integrate with existing monitoring tools.

A fundamental consideration across all deployment models is the role of agents. Agents are the workers that poll the orchestration backend for flow runs and execute them in specified environments. In Prefect Cloud, agents run anywhere with outbound internet access, abstracting worker infrastructure from orchestration concerns. Within Prefect Server and hybrid models, agents frequently execute inside Kubernetes clusters or containerized environments, enabling advanced scheduling, resource isolation, and autoscaling. Implementing custom agents can extend Prefect's execution model into specialized resource managers like Slurm or HTCondor, further expanding deployment flexibility.

From an infrastructure perspective, the resource footprint varies markedly. Prefect Cloud users are insulated from provisioning and scaling considerations, whereas Prefect Server deployments require dedicated compute, storage, and networking resources. Baseline components for Prefect Server include:

- PostgreSQL instance for metadata persistence and state tracking.

- API server, UI server, and scheduler microservices, typically containerized.

- Worker nodes or clusters capable of running distributed flows.

- Monitoring and alerting stacks, often integrated with Prometheus and Grafana.

Selecting appropriate instance sizes, storage backends, and network configurations is pivotal for performance and reliability. Horizontal scaling is primarily driven by the number of active flows and concurrency demands, with key bottlenecks often centering around the database or scheduling queue throughput.

Operationally, Prefect Cloud's managed nature simplifies upgrade management, security patching, and integration updates, while Prefect Server requires periodic manual or automated upgrades coordinated across microservice versions. Hybrid models inherit the maintenance complexity of self-hosted agents but benefit from reduced orchestration platform upgrade burdens.

Security is another axis shaping deployment choices. Prefect Cloud offers built-in encryption in transit and at rest, role-based access controls (RBAC), and compliance certifications aligned with major cloud providers. Prefect Server deployments must implement these controls manually, including TLS termination, database encryption, and audit logging configurations. Hybrid deployments introduce additional surface area, necessitating robust perimeter defenses and identity federation solutions.

The decision matrix for Prefect deployment models hinges on balancing operational overhead, customization needs, compliance, performance requirements, and total cost of ownership. Prefect Cloud accelerates adoption with minimal infrastructure burden, ideal for teams seeking immediate, scalable orchestration without administrative complexity. Prefect Server empowers organizations demanding full-stack control and customization, suitable for regulated or isolated environments. The hybrid model offers a pragmatic compromise, leveraging cloud orchestration agility while preserving execution locality and data security. Understanding the infrastructural and operational nuances of these options enables engineering teams to architect workflow orchestration solutions aligned precisely with their organizational constraints and objectives.

1.6. Security and Compliance Baseline

Effective workflow orchestration demands comprehensive security paradigms that embed authentication, authorization, and com-

pliance controls natively within the orchestration platform. Prefect integrates these critical elements to establish a robust security and compliance baseline, facilitating enterprise-grade deployments that uphold data integrity, privacy, and regulatory adherence.

Central to Prefect's security framework is *authentication*, which
ensures that every entity interacting with the orchestration system
is verified. Prefect supports token-based authentication, where
API tokens are issued and managed to enforce identity validation.
This approach eliminates implicit trust and enables fine-grained
control over access initiation. Tokens are typically scoped with expiration and privilege limits to minimize exposure risks. For environments requiring federated identity management, Prefect can
be fronted by authentication proxies or integrated with Single Sign-
On (SSO) providers, allowing enterprises to leverage existing identity stores such as LDAP, Active Directory, or OAuth2-compatible
services.

Following authentication, *authorization* governs the permissible
actions for authenticated entities within Prefect's orchestration
environment. Prefect enforces role-based access control (RBAC),
defining roles such as Administrator, Operator, and Viewer, each
mapped with specific permissions to execute, view, or administer
workflow runs and configurations. Permissions are granularly ap-
plied to different system objects, including flows, flow runs, schedules, and deployment configurations. This segregation of duties
is essential to maintain operational security and prevent privilege
escalation. Authorization policies are centrally managed and auditable, allowing administrators to align access rights with organizational security policies and compliance mandates.

Prefect also implements *secure communication protocols* to protect data in transit within the orchestration environment. Transport layer security (TLS) encrypts all client-server communications, including API calls, telemetry data, and UI interactions. This

encryption prevents interception and tampering of sensitive work-flow state information and credentials exchanged during orchestration activities. Additionally, Prefect's infrastructure components, such as agents and workers, can be configured to authenticate mutually via certificates or secure tokens, further minimizing risks related to man-in-the-middle (MitM) attacks in distributed deployments.

Data-at-rest protection considerations are vital for compliance with standards such as GDPR, HIPAA, and SOC 2. Prefect enables external storage configurations where sensitive workflow state and logs can be persisted in enterprise-grade object stores or managed databases with built-in encryption capabilities. This separation of orchestration metadata from compute nodes also simplifies adherence to data residency and retention policies. Access to stored workflow results and logs is controlled via Prefect's RBAC system and can be further restricted by integrating with cloud provider access policies or encryption key management services.

Compliance practices integrated into Prefect emphasize *auditability* and *traceability*. Every action performed within the orchestration platform is logged with detailed metadata, including user identity, timestamps, affected entities, and execution context. Prefect's audit logs can be exported to centralized logging and security information and event management (SIEM) systems, facilitating real-time monitoring, anomaly detection, and post-incident forensic analysis. These audit trails provide assurance needed for internal governance and external regulatory reviews by maintaining transparency around workflow executions and administrative changes.

To reduce operational risk, Prefect supports *policy enforcement* mechanisms, such as pre-deployment validations and runtime checks. Workflow definitions can include required security attributes, like environment variables referencing secrets manager entries, or mandates on scheduling constraints to ensure compliance with operational guidelines. Configurations are version-controlled and immutable once deployed, ensuring that workflows cannot be arbitrarily modified, which helps maintain consistent security postures over time.

Secret management within Prefect workflows complements the security baseline by abstracting sensitive information such as API keys, database credentials, and tokens. Prefect integrates with external secrets management solutions (e.g., HashiCorp Vault, AWS Secrets Manager) to retrieve secrets dynamically at runtime, minimizing hardcoded or exposed credentials in workflow code. This approach aligns with best practices for credential lifecycle management and reduces the attack surface by limiting secret exposure.

Network-level security controls augment Prefect's intrinsic mechanisms by isolating orchestration components within virtual private clouds (VPCs), restricting ingress and egress traffic based on least privilege principles. Firewalls, security groups, and routing policies ensure that workflow execution environments only communicate with authorized data sources and sinks, preserving compliance with organizational network security standards.

Prefect integrates essential security and compliance practices by embedding industry-standard authentication, authorization, encrypted communication, audit logging, and secret management directly into its workflow orchestration platform. These features set clear expectations for secure orchestration at an enterprise scale, ensuring that workflows are executed reliably without compromising critical security or compliance requirements. Enterprises deploying Prefect benefit from a baseline that supports rigorous governance and operational controls, making it suitable for highly regulated and security-sensitive environments.

Chapter 2

Programming with Prefect Core

Unlock the true potential of workflow automation by mastering Prefect's powerful yet intuitive Python-based programming model. This chapter moves beyond theory and brings you directly into the code—where expressive APIs and smart abstractions enable you to craft dynamic, resilient pipelines, tailored to your unique data and computation needs. Prepare to transform ideas into operational flows with clarity and control.

2.1. Defining Flows and Tasks Programmatically

Prefect's programmatic approach to workflow creation leverages Python's native syntax and constructs, providing a flexible and expressive platform for orchestrating complex data pipelines. Central to this approach are two primary abstractions: *tasks*, which encapsulate discrete units of work, and *flows*, which coordinate and manage the execution of one or more tasks. This section elucidates the core Prefect APIs and design patterns essential for defining and composing flows and tasks purely in code.

Tasks are designed to be Python functions or callables augmented with additional metadata and capabilities. The framework provides the @task decorator, which wraps a standard Python function, transforming it into a Prefect task object. This decorator enables Prefect to monitor task execution, handle retries, cache results, and integrate with Prefect's state management.

Consider the following example of defining a simple task that fetches data:

```
from prefect import task

@task
def fetch_data():
    # Implementation that fetches data from a database or API
    return {"key": "value"}
```

Upon decoration, fetch_data is no longer a plain Python function but a Prefect Task instance. This distinction is critical because it enables Prefect to orchestrate task execution, record task state, and inject contextual parameters when run as part of a flow.

Tasks can also specify parameters such as retries, logging behavior, and timeout durations via decorator arguments:

```
@task(retries=3, retry_delay_seconds=10)
def robust_fetch():
    # Task will retry up to 3 times with 10 seconds delay on
    failure
    pass
```

This programmatic specification allows for fine-grained control of task behavior directly within Python code.

Flows represent the orchestration layer that serializes, schedules, and executes collections of tasks. Prefect offers two principal mechanisms for flow definition: the @flow decorator and the Flow context manager.

The @flow decorator simplifies flow construction by wrapping a function that contains task invocations. Within this function, tasks are called like regular functions, but Prefect captures these calls to build the execution graph dynamically.

Example flow definition:

```
from prefect import flow

@flow
def data_pipeline():
    raw = fetch_data()
    processed = process_data(raw)
    save_results(processed)
```

Here, data_pipeline serves as the entry point of the workflow; invoking it triggers Prefect's machinery to execute the tasks fetch_data, process_data, and save_results in the appropriate order.

Alternatively, the Flow class permits explicit graph construction, which is especially useful for complex dependency management and for dynamically assembling flows:

```
from prefect import Flow

with Flow("My Flow") as flow:
    raw = fetch_data()
    processed = process_data(raw)
    save_results(processed)
```

The with block establishes the flow context, and all task invocations inside are registered as nodes in the flow's Directed Acyclic Graph (DAG). This style provides visibility into the graph structure during definition and allows attaching additional metadata or advanced configurations.

Flows construct task dependencies implicitly by capturing function call semantics. When one task's output is passed as an input parameter to another task, Prefect infers a dependency edge from the upstream to the downstream task. This data dependency model closely aligns with declarative dataflow paradigms, facilitating an intuitive mechanism for orchestrating execution order.

For example:

```
@task
def extract():
    return [1, 2, 3]

@task
def transform(data):
    return [x * 2 for x in data]

@task
def load(data):
    print(f"Loading data: {data}")

@flow
def etl_flow():
    raw_data = extract()
    transformed_data = transform(raw_data)
    load(transformed_data)
```

Here, the flow sequentially executes extract, then transform with the output from extract, and finally load with transformed data. Prefect's runtime constructs the optimal execution plan according to these input-output relationships.

Dependency edges can be manually controlled using the set_upstream and set_downstream methods on task objects if more explicit ordering is necessary, providing advanced flexibility:

```
task_a = some_task()
task_b = another_task()

task_b.set_upstream(task_a)   # task_b runs after task_a
```

However, relying on Python function call semantics for dependency management is generally preferred due to clearer readability and maintainability.

Prefect workflows often require parameterization to enable dynamic behavior based on runtime inputs. Parameters can be defined within flows using the Parameter class, which facilitates injection of external values at execution time while maintaining declarative workflow definitions.

Example of defining a parameter:

```
from prefect import Parameter

@flow
def parameterized_flow(dataset: str):
    data = fetch_data(dataset)
    process_data(data)
```

When invoking `parameterized_flow`, the caller specifies the actual dataset argument, which propagates through dependent tasks.

Tasks themselves can maintain state between runs through Prefect's built-in caching mechanisms or via explicit state handlers, aiding idempotency and optimizing pipeline re-execution. These advanced techniques involve augmenting tasks with options such as `cache_key` and `cache_expiration`, allowing Prefect to reuse intermediate results when inputs remain unchanged.

Combining tasks into modular flow components encourages reusable pipeline design. Prefect's programmatic APIs support nesting flows inside other flows, enabling hierarchical composition and encapsulation of subtasks.

For instance:

```
@flow
def preprocess_flow(raw_data):
    cleaned = clean_data(raw_data)
    validated = validate_data(cleaned)
    return validated

@flow
def main_flow():
    raw_data = fetch_data()
    clean_data = preprocess_flow(raw_data)
    analysis(clean_data)
```

By calling `preprocess_flow` within `main_flow`, a nested execution graph is formed, enhancing pipeline clarity and separation of concerns.

Additionally, looping and conditional execution constructs are supported natively by Python within flows. Tasks can be invoked in

31

loops or branches, enabling dynamic task generation and control flow:

```
@flow
def batch_processing(batch_list):
    results = []
    for batch in batch_list:
        result = process_batch(batch)
        results.append(result)
    return results
```

This general-purpose programming model grants developers the power to express intricate orchestration logic without sacrificing the benefits of Prefect's scheduling and observability.

The foundational APIs to define Prefect workflows programmatically are as follows:

- `@task`: Decorator to convert Python functions into Prefect tasks.

- `@flow`: Decorator to define flows as executable, composable workflows.

- `Flow` context manager: An alternative syntax for explicit flow graph construction.

- `Parameter`: Declarative mechanism to introduce runtime inputs.

- Task methods `set_upstream`, `set_downstream`: For manual dependency declaration.

Mastering these APIs enables the programmatic design of robust, maintainable, and scalable pipelines that leverage Prefect's full orchestration capabilities while preserving seamless integration with Python's language features.

The paradigmatic shift toward defining data workflows entirely in Python promotes pipelines that are not only reproducible and version controllable but also dynamically adaptable to evolving data contexts, operational requirements, and scaling constraints. This foundation is critical for any advanced pipeline development using Prefect.

2.2. Parameterization and Context Propagation

Effective orchestration of workflows in distributed systems hinges on the ability to dynamically adjust behavior based on runtime information. Prefect facilitates this adaptability through robust mechanisms for parameterization and context propagation, enabling flows to become versatile, data-driven constructs whose execution adapts to variable inputs and secrets without redefinition.

Parameters in Prefect flows serve as user-defined inputs whose values are supplied at execution time. This design promotes reusability and modularity by decoupling flow definitions from hardcoded constants.

A parameter is declared via the `Parameter` object within the flow context. Each parameter includes metadata such as name, default value, and optional type annotations, enhancing both readability and type safety. For example:

```
from prefect import flow, task, Parameter

@flow
def data_pipeline(date: str = Parameter("date", default
    ="2024-01-01")):
    print(f"Processing data for date: {date}")
```

When invoking the flow, different date values can be passed to control execution without editing source code. The Prefect UI and CLI expose parameter inputs, enabling operators to specify environment-specific or contextual values at runtime.

Confidential data such as API keys or passwords often must be supplied securely. Prefect integrates seamlessly with multiple secrets backends (e.g., HashiCorp Vault, AWS Secrets Manager, Kubernetes Secrets) to enable transparent secret injection.

Secrets are accessed within tasks using the prefect.context object or via Prefect's Secret utility. For example:

```
from prefect import task, flow
from prefect import get_run_context

@task
def fetch_api_data():
    context = get_run_context()
    secret_value = context.secrets.get("API_KEY")
    # Use secret_value to authenticate API calls
```

This approach abstracts secret management away from source control and disables secret exposure in logs. Prefect automatically injects secrets configured in the execution environment, allowing tasks to remain environment-agnostic.

The execution context in Prefect encapsulates environmental and runtime metadata accessible throughout flows and tasks. This context propagates key-value pairs that influence behavior dynamically.

The context object contains parameters, secrets, and additional configuration such as logging details and user-defined values. Accessing this context provides a centralized mechanism to adapt logic without explicit parameter passing into every task. The following pattern demonstrates context retrieval within a task:

```
from prefect import task, get_run_context

@task
def process_data():
    context = get_run_context()
    config_value = context.config.get("processing_threshold",
    0.8)
    # Use config_value to adjust processing logic
```

Context propagation ensures consistent configuration is maintained even when tasks execute on different agents or compute environments, preserving the integrity of the flow execution parameters.

Flows often comprise multiple tasks needing shared configuration or parameters. Passing this configuration explicitly via task inputs can become unwieldy for complex workflows. Prefect's context mechanism simplifies this by automatically propagating context to all tasks within the flow execution scope.

This implicit propagation enables tasks deep in the call graph to retrieve parameters, feature toggles, or secrets without requiring explicit plumbing. Example:

```
@flow
def training_pipeline(batch_size: int = Parameter("batch_size",
    default=64)):

    @task
    def load_data():
        context = get_run_context()
        return {"batch_size": context.parameters["batch_size"]}

    @task
    def train_model(data):
        batch_size = data["batch_size"]
        # train model with batch_size

    data = load_data()
    train_model(data)
```

Here, the `batch_size` parameter is both incorporated at flow startup and accessed seamlessly by internal tasks through the context and parameter propagation mechanism.

Developers can augment Prefect's built-in context with user-defined information to enable more sophisticated control flow and observability. This is achieved by injecting additional context values at flow start or during task execution.

Custom context allows tasks to modify downstream behavior or provide metadata for lineage, debugging, or conditional branching. Below is an example of augmenting the context in a flow:

```
from prefect import flow, task, get_run_context
from prefect.context import set_key
```

```
@flow
def enriched_context_flow():
    set_key("run_id", "abc123")

    @task
    def log_run_id():
        context = get_run_context()
        print(f"Current run id: {context.get('run_id')}")

    log_run_id()
```

Such flexibility introduces extensibility where context becomes a powerful vehicle for cross-cutting concerns in workflow execution.

Parameterization and context propagation collectively form the backbone for building data-driven workflows that adjust dynamically without code changes. By externalizing inputs and secrets, and leveraging the context for implicit configuration propagation, Prefect facilitates not only operational agility but also security and maintainability.

Flows evolve into parametrically controlled units that can operate in heterogeneous environments, incorporate user-specific or tenant-specific configuration, and react conditionally based on runtime metadata. This paradigm is indispensable for modern cloud-native orchestration at scale.

For high-complexity systems, best practices include:

- Defining all essential inputs as parameters to enable declarative invocation.

- Registering secrets securely and accessing them through Prefect's built-in secret management.

- Utilizing the context object for propagating transient or ephemeral configuration without tight coupling.

- Avoiding hardcoding configuration in task logic to maximize portability and reuse.

36

Through a disciplined use of parameterization and context propagation, workflow developers empower their orchestration layers with maximal adaptability, fostering robust, secure, and scalable automation solutions.

2.3. State Management and Transitions

Prefect's orchestration framework centers fundamentally on its state model, which governs how tasks and flows progress through their lifecycle. Understanding this model is essential for implementing robust workflows that reliably respond to successes, failures, and other runtime conditions. Each task and flow runs within a system of well-defined states, with explicit and automatic transitions enabling precise control over execution logic and error handling.

The base set of states includes `Pending`, `Running`, `Success`, `Failed`, `Skipped`, and `Retrying`, among others. When a flow or task is instantiated, it resides initially in the `Pending` state until execution begins. Transitioning to the `Running` state signifies that the work has started. From this point, the state progression depends on the outcome of execution: successful completion moves the state to `Success`, while exceptions or explicitly thrown errors trigger `Failed`, and optional retry logic may cause a shift to `Retrying` before attempting re-execution. States such as `Skipped` indicate conditional logic that bypasses task execution. States are immutable markers of execution status, ensuring reproducibility and accurate tracking.

State transitions in Prefect are predominantly automatic, driven by the internal runtime engine that monitors task and flow execution. However, Prefect provides comprehensive APIs for explicit control over these transitions. This dual approach grants users both seamless default behavior and fine-grained customizability. Explicit state management is particularly valuable for advanced use cases requiring conditional branching, external event handling, or integration of custom error recovery procedures.

Robust error recognition hinges on understanding how exceptions propagate and influence states. When a task fails due to an unhandled exception, Prefect captures the traceback and metadata, transitioning the task state to `Failed`. This failure can cascade upward and affect the parent flow state. The architecture supports retry policies, which, if configured, cause Prefect to transition the state to `Retrying` and re-submit the task execution according to specified parameters such as delay, maximum attempts, and backoff strategies.

To implement custom state-related behavior, Prefect offers the concept of state handlers. These are callback functions invoked on every state transition for a task or flow. A state handler receives the current state and the proposed next state, allowing it to inspect the results or errors and alter the transition path dynamically. State handlers facilitate a variety of use cases:

- Logging enriched context on failures.

- Triggering external alerting systems.

- Modifying retry strategies dynamically.

- Skipping downstream steps conditionally.

```
from prefect import task, Flow
from prefect.engine.state import Failed, Retrying
from datetime import timedelta

def custom_state_handler(task, old_state, new_state):
    if isinstance(new_state, Failed):
        # Log failure details
        print(f"Task {task.name} failed with: {new_state.result
}")
        # Adjust retry state dynamically
        if task.max_retries and new_state.state_count < task.
max_retries:
            return Retrying(message="Retry triggered by custom
handler")
```

```
    return new_state

@task(max_retries=2, retry_delay=timedelta(seconds=10),
    state_handlers=[custom_state_handler])
def unstable_task(x):
    if x < 0:
        raise ValueError("Negative values are not allowed")
    return x * 2

with Flow("Sample flow") as flow:
    unstable_task(-1)
```

Through explicit state inspection within a handler, one can implement complex retry policies dependent on failure types or runtime conditions. Additionally, handlers can be attached at the flow level to respond to aggregate states, such as sending notifications when any task fails or when the flow completes successfully.

State-driven logic also enables conditional branching and resilient execution paths. For example, a task downstream in a pipeline can be configured to run only if all its upstream dependencies succeeded, or alternatively, proceed with a fallback action if any upstream tasks failed. Prefect's state introspection API allows tasks to query the state of upstream tasks during runtime, thereby tailoring behavior dynamically based on real execution outcomes.

A concise example of state querying and conditional execution is shown below:

```
from prefect import task, Flow
from prefect.engine import signals

@task
def task_a():
    raise ValueError("Failure in upstream task")

@task
def task_b(upstream_state):
    if upstream_state.is_failed():
        print("Upstream failed, skipping task_b")
        raise signals.SKIP("Skipping due to upstream failure")
    return "Proceeding"

with Flow("State-aware flow") as flow:
    a_result = task_a()
    b_result = task_b(upstream_state=a_result.state)
```

In the above, task task_b checks the state of task_a and raises a skip signal if its upstream failed. Such capabilities enable workflows to be inherently resilient, adapting control flow in response to real-time error conditions without the need for manual intervention.

Prefect also integrates with external systems through its state model by emitting state change events that can be consumed by monitoring, logging, or alerting services. This capability ensures that state transitions are not only internal control mechanisms but also anchors for observability and operational insight.

Mastery of Prefect's state management and transitions is pivotal for building reliable, responsive data pipelines and automation workflows. The interplay of automatic state updates, custom state handlers, and state-driven logic constructs a powerful paradigm for detecting failure modes, implementing advanced recovery strategies, and orchestrating complex execution paths with robustness and clarity.

2.4. Custom Triggers and Advanced Control Flow

Prefect's orchestration capabilities extend far beyond basic task sequencing through the use of custom triggers and advanced control flow constructs. These mechanisms enable precise manipulation of execution logic, including conditional branching, dynamic workflow adjustments, and synchronization patterns such as fork/join. The flexibility afforded by these features allows the design of robust, responsive, and efficient data workflows aligned with complex operational requirements.

Custom Triggers for Conditional Execution

Triggers in Prefect determine whether a task should run after its upstream dependencies complete. While the default behavior is to execute a task once all upstream states are successful, custom triggers can implement sophisticated conditional logic based on those states or external conditions.

Prefect provides a variety of built-in triggers such as all_success, all_failed, any_success, and manual_only, but users can define arbitrary trigger functions by subclassing prefect.triggers.Trigger or by composing logical expressions using the prefect.triggers API.

A practical example involves executing a downstream task only if at least one upstream task succeeded, facilitating fault tolerance or partial workflow progression:

```
from prefect import task, Flow
from prefect.triggers import any_success

@task
def task_a():
    return "Result A"

@task
def task_b():
    raise ValueError("Simulated failure")

@task(trigger=any_success)
def task_c():
    return "Runs if either A or B succeeds"

with Flow("Conditional Trigger Flow") as flow:
    a = task_a()
    b = task_b()
    c = task_c(upstream_tasks=[a, b])
```

In this example, task_c executes if either task_a or task_b completes successfully, illustrating a classic fallback pattern.

Dynamic Branching via Conditional Tasks

Dynamic branching is a core requirement for workflows that adapt execution paths based on computed data or external conditions during runtime. Prefect supports this through conditional tasks

41

that programmatically decide the next steps.

The branching logic can be implemented by returning task objects or lists of tasks to indicate the path to follow, combined with conditional triggers.

Consider a use case where a flag determines which downstream path to execute:

```
from prefect import task, Flow

@task
def choose_branch(condition: bool):
    return "branch_a" if condition else "branch_b"

@task
def branch_a_task():
    return "Executed branch A"

@task
def branch_b_task():
    return "Executed branch B"

with Flow("Dynamic Branching Flow") as flow:
    condition = choose_branch(True)

    @task
    def branch_selector(branch_name):
        if branch_name == "branch_a":
            return branch_a_task()
        else:
            return branch_b_task()

    result = branch_selector(condition)
```

This pattern dynamically selects and executes the appropriate task based on an upstream decision without hardcoding static edges.

Workflow Fork and Join Patterns

Complex workflows often require parallel execution of independent tasks followed by a synchronization point that aggregates results or launches subsequent tasks. Prefect's flow design naturally supports fork/join patterns by leveraging multiple downstream edges and subsequent joins with appropriate triggers.

Parallel branches can be created by simply mapping multiple tasks from a common upstream task. Joining requires a task configured to wait for all upstream tasks to succeed (`all_success` trigger) or a custom trigger matching the desired synchronization condition.

The example below demonstrates parallel fork execution and aggregation at join:

```
from prefect import task, Flow
from prefect.engine.results import LocalResult

@task
def load_data(source):
    return f"Data from {source}"

@task
def process_data(data):
    return f"Processed {data}"

@task(trigger=prefect.triggers.all_success)
def aggregate_results(results):
    return f"Aggregated {results}"

with Flow("Fork-Join Flow") as flow:
    data_sources = ["source1", "source2", "source3"]

    raw_data = load_data.map(data_sources)
    processed = process_data.map(raw_data)
    aggregation = aggregate_results(processed)
```

Here, `load_data` and `process_data` tasks run in parallel for multiple data sources. The `aggregate_results` task joins their outputs, guaranteeing execution only after all upstream processing completes successfully.

Advanced Control Flow with Task Reruns and State Handlers

Beyond triggers and branching, Prefect allows fine-grained control through task retries and state handlers, expanding control flow semantics to incorporate failure recovery and custom state transitions.

Retries can specify maximum attempts, delay strategies, and backoff behavior to enhance workflow robustness:

```
@task(max_retries=3, retry_delay_seconds=5)
def flaky_task():
    # Task logic that may occasionally fail
    ...
```

State handlers allow intervention upon transitions such as success, failure, or completion, enabling side actions like logging, conditional triggering, or external notifications:

```
from prefect.engine.state import Failed, Success

def custom_state_handler(obj, old_state, new_state):
    if isinstance(new_state, Failed):
        print(f"Task failed: {obj.name}")
    elif isinstance(new_state, Success):
        print(f"Task succeeded: {obj.name}")
    return new_state

@task(state_handlers=[custom_state_handler])
def monitored_task():
    ...
```

This pattern permits embedding operational logic deeply into task lifecycles, yielding highly responsive workflows.

Real-World Use Case: Machine Learning Pipeline

Consider a machine learning pipeline where data preprocessing, model training, and evaluation must orchestrate conditionally and in parallel.

Using custom triggers and branching, the pipeline may execute model evaluation only if training succeeds, and in the case of failure, trigger an alert task:

```
from prefect.triggers import all_success, all_failed

@task
def preprocess_data():
    ...

@task
def train_model():
    ...

@task(trigger=all_success)
```

```
def evaluate_model():
    ...

@task(trigger=all_failed)
def alert_failure():
    ...

with Flow("ML Pipeline") as flow:
    prep = preprocess_data()
    train = train_model(upstream_tasks=[prep])
    eval_ = evaluate_model(upstream_tasks=[train])
    alert = alert_failure(upstream_tasks=[train])
```

This flow guarantees that evaluation executes only upon successful training, while a failure triggers alerting, capturing a commonly required control flow in production-level pipelines. Branching dynamically adapts the workflow, improving resilience and observability.

- **Custom triggers** provide conditional activation of tasks based on upstream states or external logic.

- **Dynamic branching** enables workflows that adapt execution paths live, creating decision-based processing.

- **Fork/join** establishes parallel execution and subsequent synchronization points with explicit triggers.

- **Retries and state handlers** enhance robustness and monitoring by embedding failure handling and state-aware controls.

Mastering these advanced control constructs within Prefect enables creation of complex yet maintainable workflows that respond dynamically to processing outcomes, failures, and external signals. This capacity is critical for scalable, production-grade automation in data-centric domains.

2.5. Retries, Timeouts, and Failure Policies

Robustness in data pipelines fundamentally depends on the ability to recover gracefully from errors, whether they are transient glitches or pervasive system faults. The architecture of such resilient workflows hinges on the carefully engineered interplay of retries, timeouts, and failure policies. These mechanisms collectively prevent cascading failures that can compromise data integrity, minimize downtime, and streamline operational costs.

Task Retry Strategies

In distributed systems, transient errors such as network hiccups, temporary service unavailability, or brief resource contention are commonplace. Retrying failed tasks judiciously can often remedy these issues without human intervention. Key considerations in retry strategy design include the number of retry attempts, backoff algorithms, and jitter to avoid systemic overloads.

The simplest retry strategy is a fixed retry count with a constant delay. However, this approach can exacerbate failure scenarios if many tasks retry simultaneously. Instead, exponential backoff is widely adopted, where the delay between retries grows exponentially, often capped by a maximum interval. Denoting the initial retry delay as d and the retry attempt number as n, the delay at attempt n is generally modeled as:

$$\text{delay}_n = \min(d \times 2^{n-1}, d_{\max})$$

where $d_{\max}$ bounds the maximum wait time. Adding random jitter, typically sampled from a uniform or Gaussian distribution, further reduces the likelihood of synchronized retry storms across distributed tasks, improving system stability.

More advanced retry strategies incorporate adaptive approaches that tailor retry timing based on task characteristics or contextual signals, such as error types or system load metrics. For instance, retries triggered by rate-limiting errors may implement longer backoffs compared to transient DNS resolution failures.

Timeout Controls

Timeouts serve as critical safeguards in workflow execution, defining maximum durations a task or operation may consume before being forcibly terminated. Properly calibrated timeouts prevent indefinite resource locking and enable timely detection of stuck or unresponsive components.

Timeouts operate at multiple granularity levels:

- **Task-level timeouts:** Limit individual task execution duration, ensuring resource reclamation if a task stalls or enters infinite loops.

- **Workflow-level timeouts:** Enforce global upper bounds on the entire workflow run, facilitating SLA adherence and operational predictability.

- **External service timeouts:** Control waits on external API calls or database queries to shield workflows from external latency spikes.

Setting timeouts requires a balance-overly aggressive values result in premature task terminations, while overly lax values inflate latency and resource consumption. Profiling typical task durations under varying conditions guides setting effective timeout thresholds.

Timeout handling often intertwines with retries. Upon timeout-triggered task failures, retry policies determine subsequent actions. Some systems enable configurable behaviors, such as immediate retry on timeout or escalation to failure policies for manual intervention.

Sophisticated Failure Policies

Failure policies codify the system response once retries are exhausted or when unrecoverable errors occur. A nuanced failure policy framework minimizes disruption while offering transparency and control options for operators and downstream processes.

Common failure policy classifications include:

1. **Fail-fast:** Workflow halts immediately upon encountering a critical failure, minimizing wasted computation and alerting operators instantaneously. This approach is suitable when errors compromise data validity or safety.

2. **Failover and fallback:** Workflow reroutes execution to alternative tasks, services, or data sources to preserve continuity despite localized failures. For example, a pipeline might switch to a cached dataset if a live data source is unreachable.

3. **Compensating actions:** Upon failure, workflows execute compensating transactions or cleanup routines to maintain system consistency. This is critical in distributed systems without atomicity guarantees.

4. **Partial success acceptance:** In some scenarios, workflows proceed despite non-critical task failures, capturing successful outputs while logging and isolating failures for later review.

Advanced workflow orchestration platforms support conditional branching based on failure status, enabling fine-grained control over alternative execution paths. Policies may integrate with alerting systems to escalate issues automatically based on severity or repeated failure patterns.

Implementation Considerations

Construction of fault-tolerant workflows is further refined by:

- **Error categorization and classification:** Distinguishing between transient, recoverable, and permanent errors allows workflows to dynamically adjust retry counts, timeouts, or switch failure strategies. For example, an error code indicating a quota exceeded scenario may trigger longer backoff compared to a syntax error, which is unlikely to be fixed by retries.

- **Idempotency:** To avoid data inconsistencies, retried tasks must ideally be idempotent. Designing idempotent tasks ensures that repeated execution, triggered by retries or failure policies, does not irreversibly alter the system state or data.

- **Stateful vs. Stateless retries:** Stateless retries, where tasks restart without reference to prior state, simplify recovery but may incur redundant computation. Stateful retries, which preserve intermediate results, can optimize resource consumption but require additional management complexity.

- **Monitoring and observability:** Effective deployment of retries and failure policies mandates comprehensive monitoring. Metrics on retry rates, timeout occurrences, and failure modes provide actionable insights to refine policies and identify systemic weaknesses.

Example: Exponential Backoff in a Data Ingestion Task

Consider a data ingestion task that intermittently fails due to temporary upstream API unavailability. Employing exponential backoff mitigates immediate retry overload:

```
import time
import random

def ingest_data():
    max_retries = 5
    base_delay = 2  # seconds
    max_delay = 30  # seconds
    for attempt in range(1, max_retries + 1):
        try:
```

```
# Attempt data ingestion
data = fetch_api_data()
process_data(data)
return True
except TransientAPIError:
    delay = min(base_delay * 2**(attempt - 1), max_delay)
    jitter = random.uniform(0, delay * 0.1)
    sleep_time = delay + jitter
    time.sleep(sleep_time)
raise RuntimeError("Failed to ingest data after retries.")
```

In this example, the delay incorporates exponential growth capped by a maximum threshold, augmented with jitter to reduce collision probability with concurrent retries.

Retries, timeouts, and failure policies are foundational to resilient workflow design, providing robust pathways for handling diverse failure scenarios. Thoughtful integration of these mechanisms, informed by empirical system behavior and error typology, transforms brittle data pipelines into adaptive, self-healing architectures capable of maintaining reliability in complex, dynamic environments.

2.6. Results Handling and Caching Strategies

Prefect's orchestration framework offers sophisticated mechanisms to manage task outputs through result storage and caching, pivotal for optimizing workflow execution. Efficient results handling enables acceleration by reducing redundant computations, supports partial recomputations when failures or modifications occur, and facilitates reproducible workload management. This section explores Prefect's result storage classes, caching policies, and the orchestration logic underpinning reuse of prior outputs.

Result Storage Abstractions

At the heart of Prefect's result handling architecture lies the Result interface, an abstraction representing persisted task outputs. Each

`Result` encapsulates metadata and data retrieval logic for a completed task. Several concrete implementations exist, supporting diverse storage backends such as local file systems, cloud object stores (AWS S3, GCS), databases, and in-memory caches. This polymorphism liberates workflows from specific storage constraints and enables seamless switching or layer combinations depending on the deployment environment.

A `Result` typically has methods to write data after task execution and to read data before task execution if caching is enabled. This dual functionality enables conditional task skips by verifying if upstream outputs exist and remain valid. For example, the `LocalResult` stores outputs as configured files:

```
from prefect.engine.results import LocalResult

local_result = LocalResult(dir="./results")
```

Serialization formats such as Pickle, JSON, or custom encoders can be combined with storage to control output persistence fidelity. The user defines the granularity of tasks whose outputs should be preserved, giving fine control over storage costs and recomputation efficiency.

Caching Mechanisms and Policies

Beyond basic result persistence, Prefect integrates caching mechanisms to intelligently reuse task outputs. Caching in Prefect revolves around two complementary concepts: task-level caching based on idempotency and parameter sensitivity, and workflow-level caching for dynamic partial recomputations.

A key component is the *cache validators*, which determine if the cached output is still valid. The common cache validators include:

- **Task Trigger**: Prefect's built-in triggers can prevent a task from running if the cached result exists.

- **Cache Key Function**: Generates a hash from task inputs

to determine if inputs have changed.

- **Maximum Cache Age**: Defines a time-to-live (TTL) after which a cached result is considered stale.

These validators can be employed in unison to handle varied scenarios. For instance, caching only occurs if the inputs are unchanged and the cache is fresher than a specified duration. This approach avoids recomputation due to side effect changes or time-dependent operations that require periodic refresh.

```
from prefect import task
from datetime import timedelta

@task(cache_key_fn=lambda task, params: hash(frozenset(params.
    items()))),
      cache_expiration=timedelta(hours=1))
def expensive_computation(param1, param2):
    # Complex operations
    return param1 * param2
```

In this snippet, the task output caching hinges on the hash of parameter combinations and expires after one hour, safeguarding against overly stale results.

Partial Recomputation and Workflow Acceleration

One of the most significant benefits of result caching is the ability to perform partial recomputations. When a workflow execution is re-triggered, Prefect consults the caching metadata to skip tasks whose outputs are still valid, thereby saving time and resources. This optimization is particularly impactful in data pipelines involving large or expensive intermediate transformations.

The workflow engine manages dependencies so that recomputation propagates downstream only when necessary. For example, if a small upstream input changes, Prefect recomputes affected tasks and downstream dependents while preserving unaffected branches.

The orchestration logic for reuse follows this sequence during runtime:

- Before running a task, Prefect queries associated result storage to check if a valid cached result exists.

- The cache validators examine input hashes, timestamps, or user-defined conditions to determine validity.

- If valid, Prefect injects the cached output as the current result, skipping task execution.

- If no valid cache exists, the task executes normally, and results are persisted for future reuse.

This process is made seamless from the user perspective, enabling efficient incremental workflow executions with minimal configuration.

Best Practices for Effective Caching

Maximizing the advantages of Prefect's caching and results handling involves careful design considerations:

- **Idempotence**: Tasks should be designed to be pure functions of their inputs to ensure reliable caching. Side effects complicate cache correctness.

- **Input Hashing Granularity**: Cache keys should reflect all significant inputs influencing computation. This includes parameters, files, and environment variables.

- **Cache Expiration**: TTLs prevent use of stale cached data, especially for data that evolves over time or depends on external systems.

- **Storage Layer Efficiency**: Use appropriate result storage based on data volume and access patterns. Cloud storage scales but incurs latency; local storage is faster but less durable.

- **Serialization Formats**: Select robust serialization methods to preserve data integrity across executions.

By adhering to these practices, workflows benefit from accelerated runtimes and robust, reproducible pipeline executions.

Integration with Prefect's UI and Monitoring

Prefect's user interface and API expose result and cache metadata, providing transparency into when tasks reuse previous outputs. Executions are annotated with cache hits or misses, allowing users to diagnose cache effectiveness and identify potential improvements.

Additionally, caching statistics assist in capacity planning and resource optimization by quantifying saved compute time versus storage overhead.

Careful leveraging of Prefect's result storage abstractions and caching strategies yields marked improvements in workflow efficiency. Persisting and reusing task outputs mitigates computational redundancy, enables scalable partial recomputations, and enhances resiliency. Mastery of these mechanisms facilitates the delivery of performant, maintainable, and cost-effective data pipelines and complex distributed workflows.

2.7. Testing and Validation of Prefect Workflows

Reliability and maintainability of data workflows hinge crucially on rigorous testing and validation. Prefect provides a robust framework to enable unit and integration testing of flows and tasks, which can be augmented with widely adopted Python testing libraries such as `pytest` and `unittest`. This section details best practices and methodologies to comprehensively validate workflow logic and task behavior, ensuring correctness, resiliency to changes, and ease of debugging.

Unit Testing Prefect Tasks

Unit tests should isolate the smallest functional units-Prefect tasks-ensuring they perform as expected independently of the flow context or external resources. Prefect tasks may wrap arbitrary user logic, so tests typically invoke the task's callable directly or through the Prefect task API.

A minimal task unit test involves calling the underlying Python function with controlled input and asserting the output matches expectations. Consider a simple task that adds two numbers:

```
from prefect import task

@task
def add(x, y):
    return x + y
```

Using `pytest`, a unit test could be:

```
def test_add():
    result = add.run(2, 3)
    assert result == 5
```

Calling `add.run()` executes the task synchronously, bypassing flow execution and scheduler logic. This approach offers simplicity and speed, facilitating rapid feedback loops.

When tasks interact with external systems-databases, APIs, or files-mocking such dependencies is essential. Python's `unittest.mock` framework or `pytest-mock` plugin allow substituting external calls with mocks or stubs to isolate task logic, reducing flakiness and runtime dependencies.

Integration Testing Flows

Integration tests validate the interaction and orchestration of multiple tasks within flows, which define dependencies and execution order. These tests verify that combined task logic performs accurately when running together and that data passing between tasks is correct.

Prefect permits synchronous execution of entire flows through the flow.run() method. This enables integration testing within a controlled environment without deploying or relying on Prefect's backend services.

Example of an integration test for a flow:

```
from prefect import flow

@task
def multiply(x, y):
    return x * y

@flow
def math_flow(a, b, c):
    sum_res = add(a, b)
    prod_res = multiply(sum_res, c)
    return prod_res

def test_math_flow():
    result = math_flow.run(2, 3, 4)
    assert result == 20  # (2 + 3) * 4
```

Such tests confirm the flow's end-to-end behavior, including task sequencing and parameter passing.

Validation of Flow Logic and Parameters

Prefect supports parameter definitions for flows and tasks, enabling dynamic and reusable workflow runs. Testing should cover parameter boundary conditions, data types, and expected failure modes.

Employ hypothesis-driven testing to generate a variety of inputs to flows, improving coverage and uncovering edge case issues. This can be combined with Prefect's flow run methods as shown:

```
from hypothesis import given, strategies as st

@given(a=st.integers(), b=st.integers(), c=st.integers())
def test_math_flow_properties(a, b, c):
    result = math_flow.run(a, b, c)
    assert isinstance(result, int)
```

Assertions should also verify task and flow states in failure cases. Prefect's state handlers or flow result inspection can be integrated into tests to assert expected exceptions or retries.

Leveraging Prefect's Testing Utilities

Prefect provides several utilities to improve testing rigor and developer experience. The `prefect.testing` module includes helpful decorators and mocks to simulate runtime environments, disable scheduling triggers, or inject test-specific configurations.

For example, using `unittest.mock.patch` to replace task calls within flows enables testing flow behavior independently of task implementations:

```
from unittest.mock import patch

@patch('module_containing_task.add')
def test_flow_with_mocked_task(mock_add):
    mock_add.return_value = 7
    result = math_flow.run(1, 2, 3)
    assert result == 21  # 7 * 3
```

This approach isolates flow orchestration logic and verifies correct handling of task outputs.

Continuous Integration and Testing Best Practices

Integrating Prefect workflow tests into automated CI pipelines ensures early detection of regressions and enforces code quality standards. Recommended practices include:

- Running all unit and integration tests on every commit using tools like `pytest`.

- Utilizing coverage tools (e.g., `coverage.py`) to track test completeness of critical workflows.

- Including static code analysis and type checking (e.g., `mypy`) alongside test suites.

- Mocking external dependencies and sensitive credentials to maintain secure and consistent test environments.

- Employing environment variable controls or Prefect context managers to toggle between testing and production configurations.

Handling Asynchronous and Scheduled Workflows

Prefect supports asynchronous tasks and schedules for periodic runs. Testing such workflows requires additional facilities to handle concurrency and timing.

One method involves invoking asynchronous tasks with `asyncio` test frameworks:

```
import asyncio
import pytest

@task
async def async_task(x):
    await asyncio.sleep(0.1)
    return x * 2

@pytest.mark.asyncio
async def test_async_task():
    result = await async_task.run(5)
    assert result == 10
```

For scheduled flows, testing should mock or bypass time-based triggers to directly invoke flow runs, preventing delays during testing cycles.

Summary of Testing Strategies

A layered testing approach maximizes robustness:

- **Unit tests** verify atomic task functions independent of flow contexts.

- **Integration tests** confirm correct composition and data flow between tasks within flows.

- **Parameter and boundary testing** validate input handling and failure modes.

- **Mocking** isolates dependencies, enabling deterministic tests.

- **Asynchronous and scheduling tests** ensure proper behavior in concurrent or time-driven scenarios.

Employing Prefect's built-in methods alongside Python testing frameworks creates an efficient and scalable validation pipeline that supports robust workflow development and maintenance.

Chapter 3

Orchestration Engine & Execution Internals

Step behind the curtain to explore the robust mechanisms that bring your Prefect workflows to life. This chapter demystifies the engine that schedules, dispatches, and manages distributed execution, providing you with the insights needed to optimize, extend, and troubleshoot your orchestrated data pipelines with confidence.

3.1. Execution Contexts: Local, Dask, and Distributed Runners

Prefect's adaptive execution architecture is designed to accommodate heterogeneous computational environments by supporting multiple execution contexts, each tailored for varying workload scales and parallelism demands. Understanding Prefect's execution contexts clarifies how workflows are dispatched, scheduled, and run on particular backends and resource models. This section delves into the nuances and practical implications of three primary execution contexts: Local Runners, Dask Runners, and Distributed Runners.

Local Execution Context

The Local Runner provides the most fundamental execution model in Prefect. It is primarily single-threaded and synchronous, operating within the runtime environment where the Prefect orchestration process is initiated. This execution context is tightly coupled with the Python process executing the flow, making it ideal for development, testing, and workflows with lightweight computational demands or dependencies on local resources.

Local execution invokes task runs immediately upon the scheduler's action, directly blocking the flow's progress until the current task completes. Although task concurrency is limited by the Python runtime's inherent single-threaded nature (or constrained by the Global Interpreter Lock, GIL), the Local Runner offers straightforward debugging and minimal infrastructure overhead. It thereby serves as the foundational execution context upon which more complex strategies build.

Parallel Execution with Dask

To overcome the limitations of sequential execution and harness parallelism on multi-core machines or clusters, Prefect integrates seamlessly with the Dask ecosystem. The Dask Runner facilitates parallel task execution by leveraging a Dask scheduler, which orchestrates task distribution and workload balancing across multiple workers.

Dask achieves this by constructing a directed acyclic graph (DAG) representing task dependencies and enqueuing them to a distributed or local thread/process scheduler. Prefect's Dask Runner initializes and connects to this scheduler, providing a conduit through which Prefect tasks are submitted as Dask futures.

A representative code snippet configuring a Dask-based Prefect flow would appear as follows:

```
from prefect import Flow, task
from prefect.executors import DaskExecutor

@task
def increment(x):
    return x + 1

with Flow("dask-parallel") as flow:
    results = increment.map([1, 2, 3, 4])

flow.executor = DaskExecutor()
flow.run()
```

Here, the use of DaskExecutor allows parallel evaluation of the mapped increment tasks across available Dask workers. The Dask Runner's strength lies in dynamic resource allocation and support for both local threads/processes and remote cluster modes (via Dask distributed scheduler).

Dask also enables advanced features such as task-level retries, resource constraints, and adaptive scaling, useful when handling computationally intensive workflows with complex parallelism patterns. For example, launching a Dask cluster on Kubernetes or cloud instances provides elastic scalability while maintaining consistent Prefect orchestration semantics.

Distributed Execution for Scalability

Executions at large scale necessitate a distributed execution context beyond local multi-threading or process-based parallelism. While Dask can operate in distributed modes, Prefect extends this concept with explicit Distributed Runners that manage task execution over clusters spanning multiple physical or virtual machines.

Distributed Runners in Prefect encapsulate interaction with cluster resource managers, message brokers, and third-party distributed task queues. They introduce abstractions to dispatch, monitor, retry, and collect results asynchronously over networked environments. This setup unleashes horizontal scalability by decoupling task execution from orchestration and state management components.

Examples of distributed execution contexts include:

- *Kubernetes Executors*: Tasks run as isolated Pods coordinated via the Kubernetes API, harnessing cluster autoscaling and resource quotas.

- *Cloud-managed Distributed Systems*: Integrations with managed services such as AWS Batch, Google Cloud Dataflow, or Azure Batch, abstracting the provisioning of virtual clusters.

- *Message Broker-Based Architectures*: Employing message queues like RabbitMQ or Apache Kafka to distribute task messages asynchronously across worker instances.

These environments typically deploy Prefect Agents or Runners that continuously poll for scheduled flows and instantiate task containers, worker processes, or serverless functions accordingly. Prefect's state management ensures transparent propagation of task states and robust failure handling across machines.

Distributed execution contexts optimize workloads characterized by:

- Large-scale data processing or machine learning pipelines requiring thousands of concurrent tasks.

- Heterogeneous resource requirements demanding specialized hardware (e.g., GPUs) or isolation.

- Highly available production systems needing resilient recovery from node failures or preemptions.

Comparative Analysis and Use Cases

Execution Context	Characteristics and Use Cases
Local Runner	Best suited for development, debugging, and low-throughput workflows. No external dependencies, runs synchronously in a single Python process.
Dask Runner	Enables parallelism on a single machine or cluster, excels at CPU-bound or IO-bound tasks. Suitable for workflows benefiting from task-level concurrency and lightweight scaling.
Distributed Runner	Designed for large-scale, multi-node infrastructures requiring horizontal scalability, fault tolerance, and integration with cloud or cluster resource managers. Ideal for high-throughput production workloads.

The choice of execution context directly influences task scheduling latency, resource utilization efficiency, and fault recovery models. Local execution sacrifices scalability for simplicity; Dask balances parallelism and resource economy, while distributed contexts prioritize scalability and resilience at the expense of increased operational complexity.

Execution Flow and State Management Across Contexts

Regardless of the execution context, Prefect maintains uniform orchestration semantics through consistent state management. Each task's state transitions (e.g., `Pending`, `Running`, `Failed`, `Success`) are tracked via the Prefect backend or API, enabling monitoring, retries, and dynamic branching independent of the underlying executor.

Importantly, task inputs and outputs may be serialized, sent over network boundaries, or accessed via artifact stores to support distributability. Prefect abstracts these logistics, allowing authors to focus on workflow logic rather than infrastructure coordination.

Effective Prefect flow execution demands selecting an appropriate runner that matches the operational context:

- **For local iterative development**, choose the Local Runner to simplify debugging cycles.

- **For medium-scale parallel tasks** on shared compute resources or dedicated clusters, leverage the Dask Runner.

- **For large-scale production environments** with significant concurrency, heterogeneity, and fault tolerance requirements, deploy Distributed Runners integrated with cluster and cloud orchestration systems.

An understanding of these execution modalities enables architects and engineers to optimize resource usage while maintaining Prefect's declarative and composable workflow abstractions.

3.2. Task Scheduling and Concurrency Management

Prefect's architecture for task scheduling and concurrency management is designed to maximize resource utilization while maintaining robust execution guarantees. At its core, Prefect implements a decentralized execution model that orchestrates task runs through a combination of event-driven scheduling, intelligent queuing, and isolation primitives that permit both parallelism and fault tolerance.

Task scheduling in Prefect operates by first decomposing workflows into discrete units of work, referred to as tasks, which are dispatched to an execution context. These tasks are submitted to task queues managed by Prefect agents, which communicate with the Prefect backend. Each task is associated with metadata including priority, retry policies, dependencies, and resource requirements. Prefect's scheduler prioritizes task execution according to a directed acyclic graph (DAG) structure, honoring dependency constraints to ensure correctness. The scheduler traverses the DAG, identifying runnable tasks whose upstream dependencies have completed successfully and enqueues them for execution.

Inside the Prefect agent environment, tasks are maintained in internal priority queues that respect these dependencies and metadata. Prefect supports configurable task prioritization schemes

66

whereby tasks with higher business or computational priority pre-empt others, allowing critical paths to be expedited. The priority queues facilitate seamless scaling by dynamically adjusting to changes in workload and resource availability.

Prefect's concurrency model exploits both thread-level and process-level parallelism. This dual isolation strategy provides flexibility across heterogeneous execution environments, whether running on local machines or distributed cloud infrastructure. Thread-based concurrency is typically employed for lightweight or I/O-bound tasks, where thread pools manage concurrent execution without the overhead of process context switching. In contrast, CPU-bound or potentially unstable tasks are executed in separate processes using process pools. This process-level isolation mitigates risks of memory leaks or segmentation faults impacting the scheduler or other tasks.

Prefect leverages Python's standard `concurrent.futures` module as a foundation for concurrency primitives, extending it for fine-grained control over task lifecycle and state tracking. The agent maintains pools of threads and processes with dynamic capacity, scaling according to configured concurrency limits and observed throughput. These pools execute task functions asynchronously, while concurrently monitoring task states and handling preemption or retries.

Synchronization between concurrent tasks is handled through Prefect's internal event-driven messaging system combined with concurrency primitives such as locks, semaphores, and condition variables. These primitives protect shared resources and coordinate critical sections to prevent race conditions. Prefect's runtime engine ensures that task state transitions-such as RUNNING, SUCCESS, FAILURE-are atomic and consistently propagated through the system, enabling external observers and monitoring tools to maintain accurate task status views.

When deploying on cloud or containerized environments, Prefect orchestrates concurrency across multiple nodes and containers by using distributed task queues backed by message brokers such as RabbitMQ or Redis. This approach decouples task producers from consumers, enhancing scalability and fault tolerance. Prefect agents poll these queues, fetching tasks according to availability and priority. Cloud-native concurrency management further leverages auto-scaling clusters, dynamically increasing processing capacity when demand spikes, while respecting concurrency limits to avoid resource exhaustion.

Task retries and backoff strategies integrate tightly with the concurrency model. Prefect supports configurable retry policies with exponential backoff, jitter, and maximum retry counts. Failed tasks are re-queued with adjusted priority and delay parameters, preventing continuous contention for resources and enabling graceful recovery from transient errors. The scheduler's adherence to a declarative task state machine ensures that retries do not violate dependency constraints or cause deadlocks.

Logging and telemetry are integral to Prefect's concurrency management architecture. Each task execution records detailed event streams capturing start times, resource usage, completion status, and errors. These logs enable dynamic scheduling adjustments based on historical task performance, such as re-prioritizing consistently slow tasks or reallocating concurrency quotas. Prefect's observability framework thus empowers operators to tune schedules, concurrency limits, and resource allocations to balance throughput, latency, and cost.

The following code snippet illustrates a conceptual example of Prefect's concurrency primitives managing a set of tasks with dependencies and retry policies:

```
from prefect import task, Flow
from prefect.engine.state import Failed

@task(max_retries=3, retry_delay_seconds=10)
def process_data(x):
    if x % 2 == 0:
```

```
        raise ValueError("Simulated failure for even numbers")
    return x * 2

@task
def finalize(results):
    return sum(results)

with Flow("concurrent-flow") as flow:
    results = []
    for i in range(5):
        r = process_data(i)
        results.append(r)
    total = finalize(results)
```

In this example, tasks represented by process_data run concurrently, leveraging Prefect's thread/process pools. Failures trigger retries using the defined policy, and successful outputs feed into the finalize task once all upstream dependencies complete. Prefect's scheduler ensures correct ordering and concurrency, automatically isolating task executions to prevent interference between retries and parallel tasks.

Overall, Prefect's task scheduling and concurrency management combine prioritized queuing, dependency-aware orchestration, isolated execution contexts, and cloud-scalable distributed queues to achieve efficient and reliable workflow execution. This design balances the complex tradeoffs between parallelism, resource constraints, fault tolerance, and observability, enabling sophisticated data engineering and machine learning workflows to run predictably in diverse environments.

3.3. Flow Serialization, Storage Backends, and Transport

In Prefect, the orchestration of workflows across diverse computational environments necessitates sophisticated mechanisms for packaging, serializing, storing, and transporting both code and state artifacts. The core challenge addressed by these mechanisms is ensuring that a defined flow, along with its runtime context, artifacts, and dependencies, can be securely and efficiently executed remote from its origin while preserving reproducibility and minimizing latency.

Flow Serialization Prefect employs an advanced serialization approach where the flow object, including all tasks, parameters, and associated state information, is converted into a JSON-compatible structure through a process known as *flow serialization*. This process uses Prefect's custom serialization schema, which extends native JSON encoding by accommodating Python-specific constructs such as function references, task configurations, and complex nested objects. By leveraging `cloudpickle` under the hood, Prefect ensures that arbitrary Python code segments-such as user-defined functions or callable tasks-are serialized into byte streams that capture their logic and closure variables.

The output of serialization is a deterministic and comprehensive snapshot representing the executable graph structure and configuration metadata. This snapshot facilitates flow execution environments to reconstruct the flow programmatically without requiring source-level access or redevelopment, thus enabling distributed and fault-tolerant orchestration.

Flow Package Creation and Artifact Assembly Beyond serialization, Prefect supports the bundling of flow-related artifacts into transportable packages known as *Flow Packages*. These packages aggregate serialized flow definitions, dependency specifications, environment variables, and ancillary files-such as scripts or resource manifests-that are essential for execution fidelity. Packaging is typically performed via a utility that collates the serialized flow JSON alongside additional resource files into well-defined archive formats compliant with storage backend requirements.

This modular packaging approach provides flexibility for deploying flows across heterogeneous cloud and on-premise compute clusters. It decouples code development from execution infrastructure, fostering portability and version control of orchestrated workflows.

Distributed Storage Backends Storage backends serve as critical intermediaries enabling persistence and retrieval of flow packages and runtime states at scale. Prefect natively integrates with a broad array of distributed storage solutions, including but not limited to Amazon S3, Google Cloud Storage, Azure Blob Storage, and traditional object stores compatible with the S3 protocol. The choice of backend hinges on organizational ecosystem alignment, scalability demands, data governance policies, and access latency considerations.

Files and serialized artifacts stored in such backends are typically organized under unique namespace prefixes or bucket paths linked to flow identifiers and execution timestamps. This systematic storage hierarchy facilitates flow versioning, auditability, and rollback capabilities. Prefect's storage interface abstracts the backend-specific APIs, providing a uniform method to upload, fetch, and manage flow packages regardless of the underlying storage technology.

Secure and Efficient Artifact Transport Transport of flow packages from storage backends to execution environments (agents or workers) is engineered for security and efficiency. Prefect ensures data integrity and confidentiality through the use of encrypted transport protocols (such as HTTPS or SSH tunnels) during artifact fetch operations. Additionally, authentication mechanisms-such as AWS IAM roles, OAuth tokens, or service principal credentials-are employed to restrict unauthorized access to sensitive code and data.

To optimize the transport pipeline, Prefect incorporates several strategies:

- **Incremental Sync and Caching**: Agents cache frequently

used packages locally to minimize redundant downloads, particularly for repeated flow executions or retried runs.

- **Compressed Archives**: Flow packages are compressed to reduce payload size and network bandwidth utilization.

- **Parallel Streaming**: Artifact downloads leverage concurrent stream pipelines where supported, accelerating ingestion in bandwidth-rich environments.

Such optimizations are paramount for large-scale orchestrations where minimizing startup latency directly impacts overall workflow throughput and system responsiveness.

Integration with Execution Environments Upon receipt of the flow package, execution agents utilize the serialized definitions to instantiate runtime flow objects that mirror the original design-time structure. Agents unpack artifacts from storage, decompress if necessary, and deserialize JSON payloads into in-memory task graphs. Prefect's runtime leverages this reconstructed context to schedule tasks, manage dependencies, and propagate state transitions seamlessly.

This model supports hybrid environments encompassing containerized Kubernetes clusters, virtual machines, or managed serverless compute, as execution dependencies and environmental configurations travel alongside code artifacts within the packaged flows. Such cohesion allows Prefect to abstract the complexities of environment heterogeneity, presenting a consistent execution paradigm to users.

The combination of reliable flow serialization, flexible packaging, integration with robust distributed storage backends, and secure transport channels embodies the cornerstone of Prefect's architecture for scalable workflow management. This paradigm ensures that flows can be defined once, persistently stored, and executed anywhere with guaranteed fidelity, security, and operational efficiency-thus enabling advanced use cases in data engineering, machine learning pipelines, and automated process orchestration on an enterprise scale.

3.4. Prefect Agents, Work Pools, and Executors

Prefect's architecture for scalable and dynamic workflow execution relies fundamentally on a distributed agent model. This model provides the structural underpinnings to manage resource provisioning, task scheduling, and workload distribution across a variety of execution environments. The interplay between agents, work pools, and executors enables Prefect to adapt resource allocation in real time, balancing loads efficiently to meet the demands of complex, large-scale pipelines.

Agents: Provisioning and Lifecycle

Agents in Prefect serve as the active intermediaries bridging the Prefect Cloud or Prefect Server orchestration layer with specific compute environments. They are responsible for monitoring work pools and provisioning the execution of flow runs by spinning up or delegating tasks onto available resources.

Each agent instance continuously polls the Prefect API for work items from work pools it is configured to monitor. Upon receiving a flow run, the agent orchestrates the instantiation of the execution environment, whether that be a container, virtual machine, or a native environment on a host system. Agents can be configured for diverse infrastructure targets such as Kubernetes clusters, cloud virtual machines (e.g., AWS EC2, Google Compute Engine), Docker hosts, or local machines.

The lifecycle of an agent execution can be summarized as follows:

1. Polling: Agents regularly query the Prefect backend to discover available flow runs in their subscribed work pools.

2. Acquisition: Agents acquire a flow run lease, preventing other agents from picking the same work.

3. Execution Provisioning: The agent launches the appropriate environment for the flow run, injecting environment variables, secrets, and any required configurations.

4. Execution Monitoring: While the flow run executes, the agent streams logs and status updates back to the Prefect backend.

5. Completion and Cleanup: Upon completion, the agent releases the lease, cleans up resources if temporary, and resumes polling for further work.

The distributed and loosely coupled nature of agents supports fault tolerance. If an agent fails during execution, the backend automatically detects lease expiration, enabling other agents to resume the work, thereby providing high availability.

Work Pools: Defining the Execution Resource Domains

Work pools act as logical groupings of compute resources and represent queues of work waiting to be processed by agents. When a flow is scheduled for execution, it is assigned to a particular work pool, effectively determining the environment and infrastructure that will process the workload.

From a configuration standpoint, work pools embody metadata such as their infrastructure type (e.g., Kubernetes, Docker, Process), concurrency limits, tagging for workload classification, and provisioning arguments specific to the infrastructure runtime-such as node selectors in Kubernetes or resource limits for Docker containers.

- *Concurrency Controls*: Work pools allow administrators to limit the number of concurrent executions, preventing resource overcommitment and enabling fine-tuning for diverse environments.

- *Tagging and Priority*: Work pools can be tagged with metadata, which agents use to filter applicable flows. This facilitates the prioritization of workloads and the segregation of different flow execution types (e.g., batch jobs vs. streaming).

- *Dynamic Scaling*: When combined with cloud APIs or orchestration platforms, work pools can trigger autoscaling behaviors. For example, a Kubernetes-based work pool can dynamically provision new pods in response to increased workflow demand.

This abstraction decouples workflow definitions from specific infrastructure, enabling operational flexibility. Developers specify which work pool a flow should employ, but the underlying agents and executors handle resource management transparently.

Executors: Controlling Task Concurrency and Execution Patterns

Executors dictate the concurrency models and execution semantics within the compute environment provisioned by an agent. While agents manage resource provisioning, executors define how flow runs and individual tasks execute once the runtime environment is ready.

Prefect offers a variety of executor implementations, each suited to different operational contexts:

- *LocalExecutor*: Runs flow runs locally in threads or processes, suitable for development or lightweight tasks where isolation is not critical.

- *DaskExecutor*: Integrates with Dask clusters, distributing task executions over multiple nodes or cores, providing robust parallelization and load balancing.

- *ConcurrentExecutor*: Executes tasks concurrently using Python's concurrency interfaces, optimizing CPU utilization within a single process.

- *Custom Executors*: Users may implement customized executor logic to suit unique distributed systems or specialized resource managers.

Executors expose configuration parameters that govern concurrency limits, task retries, and scheduling policies. For example, the DaskExecutor leverages Dask's scheduler to dynamically balance workloads, minimize idle time, and redistribute tasks in the event of node failures.

Dynamic Resource Management and Load Balancing

Together, agents, work pools, and executors form a hierarchical framework enabling dynamic resource management:

- Discovery and Leasing: Agents monitor work pools to discover pending flow runs and acquire leases to execute the work, ensuring exclusive ownership and preventing duplicate executions.

- Provisioning: Based on the work pool configuration, agents instantiate suitable compute environments. This step is enhanced by integration with orchestration platforms capable of autoscaling and resource lifecycle management.

- Execution: Executors within the provisioned environment schedule and run tasks, leveraging concurrent execution where applicable.

- Health Monitoring: Agents persistently monitor running executions and report status updates to the orchestration backend, enabling retry mechanisms or failover when necessary.

This model ensures seamless workload balancing by distributing execution demand across available agents and compute resources.

When demand surges, additional agents can be deployed, or existing agents can scale their work pools' resources, maintaining throughput without manual intervention.

Illustrative Agent Configuration Example

A Kubernetes agent definition, for instance, may specify the image, namespace, service account, and resource requests to enable autoscaling in a cluster:

```
apiVersion: apps/v1
kind: Deployment
metadata:
  name: prefect-agent
spec:
  replicas: 3
  selector:
    matchLabels:
      app: prefect-agent
  template:
    metadata:
      labels:
        app: prefect-agent
    spec:
      containers:
        - name: agent
          image: prefecthq/prefect:latest
          args: ["agent", "kubernetes", "start", "--work-pool", "
my-k8s-pool"]
          resources:
            requests:
              cpu: "500m"
              memory: "512Mi"
            limits:
              cpu: "1"
              memory: "1Gi"
```

The above example highlights how agents can be configured declaratively, aligning with Kubernetes practices and ensuring that scaling and orchestration infrastructure can manage resource utilization responsively.

The distributed agent model in Prefect, combined with work pools and executors, provides a robust architecture for scalable workflow execution. By abstracting resource provisioning and task scheduling into modular components, Prefect supports heterogeneous infrastructure, dynamic scaling, and resilient workload balancing. This design empowers users to create sophisticated, high-throughput data pipelines that can adjust resource consumption based on real-time demand and operational constraints, yielding efficient and fault-tolerant distributed execution.

3.5. Event-driven Orchestration and Triggers

Event-driven orchestration transforms pipeline execution by enabling workflows to respond dynamically to various internal and external events rather than following strictly linear, time-driven schedules. Prefect's architecture offers powerful constructs to seamlessly implement event-driven triggers, facilitating reactive, adaptive, and efficient data workflows tailored for modern event streaming and callback-intensive environments.

At the core of Prefect's event-driven orchestration lies the concept of *task triggers*, which determine whether a task should run based on the outcomes or signals from preceding tasks or external inputs. Unlike conventional task execution strategies that rely solely on success or failure conditions, Prefect extends this model by supporting custom trigger functions. These functions enable developers to programmatically control task activation, exploring intricate conditional logic that can incorporate success, failure, skipped runs, timeouts, or even external signals embedded as state metadata.

Formally, a trigger in Prefect is a callable that receives information about the upstream task states and outputs a boolean indicating whether the target task should commence execution. This abstraction supports scenarios such as:

- Conditional branching based on the success of specific upstream tasks combined with exclusion criteria tied to other task states.

78

- Triggering retries or compensating tasks upon failure by activating alternate workflow branches.

- Initiating task runs only if external signals, such as webhook callbacks or message queue notifications, are received and verified.

To build truly responsive, non-linear workflows, Prefect allows these triggers to be composed with orchestration control flow constructs (e.g., mapped tasks, loops, conditional branching). For example, one can construct a reactive pipeline where data ingestion tasks execute only after an external file arrival event is detected, followed by dynamic branching that processes different data types based on metadata attributes extracted at runtime.

Integration with external event streaming platforms and callback-based systems is facilitated through Prefect's extensible event-handling interfaces. Prefect flows can be instrumented with sensors-special constructs designed to await specific events or messages, such as the arrival of a Kafka message, completion of an API call, or detection of a file modification in a cloud storage bucket. These sensors act as asynchronous triggers that pause or initiate portions of a workflow contingent on real-world signals.

For instance, implementing a Kafka event sensor involves consuming messages from a topic and transforming these into Prefect task signals by leveraging Prefect's Python client and state-setting APIs. Consider the following simplified example of a Kafka sensor trigger embedded within a Prefect flow:

```
from prefect import task, Flow, triggers
from confluent_kafka import Consumer

def kafka_event_trigger(upstream_states):
    # Only trigger if a message was received in external Kafka
    poll
    for state in upstream_states:
        if state.is_successful() and state.result == 'new_event':
            return True
    return False
```

```
@task
def poll_kafka_topic():
    consumer = Consumer({
        'bootstrap.servers': 'broker:9092',
        'group.id': 'prefect_group',
        'auto.offset.reset': 'earliest'
    })
    consumer.subscribe(['data_topic'])
    msg = consumer.poll(timeout=5.0)
    if msg is None:
        return None
    elif msg.error():
        raise RuntimeError(msg.error())
    else:
        return 'new_event'

@task(trigger=kafka_event_trigger)
def process_event():
    # Process data upon event detection
    pass

with Flow("EventDrivenFlow") as flow:
    event_signal = poll_kafka_topic()
    process_event(upstream_tasks=[event_signal])
```

This example illustrates how a single task, `poll_kafka_topic`, listens for new Kafka messages and, upon detecting a qualifying event, triggers a downstream processing task using a custom trigger function. Such integration patterns unlock the ability to synchronize complex pipelines with external asynchronous data streams efficiently.

Another common pattern involves webhooks or callback mechanisms. Prefect can host lightweight HTTP endpoints or integrate with function-as-a-service (FaaS) platforms to receive push notifications that dynamically activate workflow components. The callback payload is ingested, verified, and used to update task states or trigger downstream tasks. This on-demand orchestration drastically reduces idling resources and accelerates response times.

Prefect's state management and logging infrastructure further augment event-driven capabilities by capturing and propagating event metadata. This metadata-driven control flow can be harnessed to implement fine-grained event correlation and historical auditing.

Events from multiple heterogeneous sources can be combined to trigger composite conditional executions, enabling robust orchestration across distributed systems.

Furthermore, Prefect supports event-driven scheduling by coupling triggers with its scheduling API. Pipelines can be configured to run not only on fixed intervals but also whenever specific external events occur. This hybrid approach blends time-based and event-based orchestration, catering to scenarios requiring timely responses with fallback regular executions.

Prefect's event-driven triggers and orchestration mechanisms empower the design of workflows that are intrinsically reactive to internal task states and external signals. The ability to define custom triggers coupled with sensor constructs enables intricate control over pipeline progression, allowing operational logic to follow business events and asynchronous data flows natively. Such patterns are essential in building modern data pipelines that integrate with cloud-native event streaming systems, event-driven microservices, and real-time callback frameworks, ensuring pipelines remain efficient, resilient, and responsive.

3.6. Observability: Logging, Monitoring, and Instrumentation

Achieving robust observability in workflow automation is fundamental for understanding system behavior, troubleshooting failures, and optimizing performance. Prefect integrates comprehensive telemetry, logging, and metrics tools that enable detailed insights into the execution of data flows. These features support collection of execution traces, real-time monitoring, and instrumentation for diagnostics and automated reporting, forming the backbone of effective operational visibility and control.

Telemetry in Prefect captures detailed events emitted at various stages of a flow and task lifecycle. Each event includes metadata such as timestamps, identifiers, statuses, and contextual information, enabling end-to-end traceability. This trace data helps reconstruct the execution path and timing relationships, crucial for root cause analysis, performance profiling, and anomaly detection.

The Prefect architecture leverages a centralized metadata store that continuously aggregates telemetry data streamed from flow runners. Incorporating distributed tracing standards, Prefect's telemetry correlates parent and child task executions, capturing causal dependencies within complex workflows. Developers can integrate Prefect traces with external observability platforms by exporting telemetry via standardized protocols or APIs, facilitating unified cross-service diagnostics.

Logging is indispensable for capturing granular runtime information, error diagnostics, and audit trails. Prefect implements structured logging, where each log entry is associated with flow or task identifiers and enriched with metadata such as log level, hostname, and thread details.

Users can configure logging behavior programmatically or declaratively via the Prefect configuration system, enabling control over log verbosity and format. Logs are emitted to multiple sinks including local files, standard output, or remote services compatible with log aggregation tools like ELK (Elasticsearch, Logstash, Kibana) or Fluentd.

Prefect also supports log streaming in real-time during flow execution, providing immediate visibility into task progress and potential issues. This capability facilitates operational responsiveness, allowing for rapid intervention or automated alerting based on specific logged events or error patterns.

Monitoring workflow execution in real-time is pivotal for operational awareness and management. Prefect includes a web-based UI and API endpoints that present live status updates on flow runs, task states, and resource consumption metrics.

Key performance indicators such as task duration, success/failure rates, queue times, and retries are continuously aggregated and visualized through customizable dashboards. This metric data enables identification of bottlenecks, capacity issues, and irregularities in scheduling or execution patterns.

To support integrations with external monitoring and alerting frameworks (e.g., Prometheus, Grafana), Prefect exposes metrics via dedicated endpoints or exporters. Adopting standard metrics formats facilitates seamless ingestion into enterprise monitoring ecosystems. Aggregated metrics combined with historical logs and traces give rise to a comprehensive observability stack, enabling predictive analytics and proactive incident management.

Instrumenting workflows and tasks with custom metrics and diagnostic probes enhances observability beyond default telemetry. Prefect allows embedding instrumentation directly within flow code through lightweight APIs that emit user-defined metrics, events, or annotations.

This granular instrumentation empowers developers to capture domain-specific indicators such as data quality measures, business logic checkpoints, or system resource usage. Such rich semantic context accelerates fault isolation and operational intelligence.

Prefect's instrumentation integrates with notification systems and automated reporting tools, enabling workflows to generate actionable insights upon completion or failure. For example, summary reports containing execution statistics, error contexts, or generated artifacts can be auto-published to dashboards, messaging platforms, or ticketing systems.

Maximizing observability benefits requires deliberate integration strategies:

- **Unified Context Propagation:** Ensure telemetry and

logs consistently propagate contextual metadata (flow ID, task ID, run ID) to correlate related events across the observability stack.

- **Adaptive Logging Levels:** Implement dynamic log level controls to balance verbosity and performance overhead, allowing detailed diagnostic data during debugging and succinct logs in production.

- **Instrumentation Standardization:** Define and reuse common instrumentation conventions and metric schemas to simplify analysis and aggregation across multiple workflows.

- **Automation of Alerting and Reporting:** Couple observability with alert rules and scheduled reports to enable rapid response and continuous operational improvement.

Incorporating Prefect's telemetry, logging, and metrics capabilities creates an integrated observability framework essential for scaling and operating complex automated workflows. This framework not only illuminates execution details but also empowers data-driven decision-making and resilient system management.

Chapter 4

Workflow Reliability, Scalability, and Performance

Unlock the secrets to building resilient and performant pipelines that stand the test of scale and volatility. This chapter explores practical and advanced techniques to keep your workflows reliable under failure, highly available in production, and efficient as your data and operations grow. Get ready to architect solutions that consistently deliver results—no matter the size, speed, or complexity.

4.1. Designing for Idempotence and Fault Tolerance

Idempotence and fault tolerance are foundational principles in constructing resilient workflows, especially in distributed and large-scale data processing systems. Ensuring that tasks and entire workflows can be safely re-executed without adverse side effects is critical to robustness. Similarly, the ability to detect, isolate, and recover from errors without cascading failures guarantees business continuity and consistency. Prefect, as a workflow orchestration framework, provides essential abstractions and tools that facilitate the design of idempotent and fault-tolerant pipelines.

Idempotence: Definition and Importance

Idempotence refers to the property of an operation wherein executing it multiple times produces the same effect as executing it once. In the context of workflows, an idempotent task or process can be retried or re-run-due to failure or manual invocation-without introducing inconsistencies such as corrupted data, duplicated outputs, or side effects like double billing.

Achieving idempotence requires careful consideration of both task logic and external interactions:

- **Immutable Inputs:** Tasks should avoid reliance on mutable external state unless managed transactionally. Instead, tasks ideally consume explicitly versioned or timestamped data, which guarantees reproducibility.

- **Atomic Side Effects:** When a task affects an external system (e.g., writing to a database or posting to a message queue), the operation must either be atomic or detect and reconcile duplicates.

- **Deterministic Outputs:** Ensuring that the same input consistently yields the same output is crucial. Non-determinism (e.g., use of random seeds or timestamps) must be controlled or factored explicitly into idempotence strategies.

Designing idempotent tasks allows Prefect's retry mechanisms and

86

checkpointing to re-execute only the failed or incomplete parts of a flow safely, enhancing system reliability.

Error Handling Strategies within Prefect

Graceful error handling complements idempotence by enabling workflows to recover or alert based on transient or permanent failures. Prefect provides multiple constructs to manage errors explicitly:

- **Automatic Retries:** Tasks can be decorated with retry policies, specifying the number of retries, delay intervals, and backoff strategies. Prefect's built-in retry logic helps overcome transient issues such as network interruptions or temporary resource unavailability.

- **Failure Hooks and States:** Prefect allows registration of callbacks to respond to failure events or specific state transitions. These hooks can perform operations like logging, cleanup, notification, or triggering compensating workflows.

- **Result Handlers:** Intermediate results can be persisted outside volatile environments to enable resumption from checkpoints, reducing wasted computation on recoverable errors.

- **Conditional Branching and Timeouts:** Flows may include logic to branch based on the success or failure of previous tasks or abort execution after defined timeouts, preventing cascading resource consumption.

These mechanisms promote defensive programming, explicit control flow, and observability, empowering operators to anticipate and mitigate failure modes.

Patterns for Building Durable and Repeatable Processes

Several core design patterns emerge for constructing resilient workflows with Prefect:

Checkpointing and State Persistence

Prefect supports state handlers that save task outputs to storage backends such as cloud object stores or databases. Persisting intermediate results enables the restart of flows from last successful states without recomputing the entire pipeline. This pattern is particularly effective for long-running workflows or those involving expensive computations.

Idempotent External Effects

When interacting with external APIs or services, wrappers or adapters enforce idempotency by including unique request identifiers or leveraging idempotency keys supported by the external system. For instance, writing to an API with a unique idempotency token ensures repeated requests do not create duplicate entries.

Compensating Transactions

In workflows that perform multi-step updates to heterogeneous systems, failures may occur mid-process. Prefect flows can incorporate compensating tasks-designed to rollback or neutralize partial changes-to restore consistency. These tasks execute conditionally on failure states, implementing a controlled undo paradigm.

Timeouts and Circuit Breakers

Introducing timeouts on tasks precludes indefinite hangs. Coupled with circuit breaker logic, which halts retry attempts after repeated failures, flows avoid resource exhaustion. Prefect's task decorators allow specification of timeout durations and custom state transitions on timeout events.

Dynamic Task Mapping with Granularity Control

Task mapping enables execution of parallel instances operating on partitioned data. Maintaining idempotence at this fine granularity limits re-execution scope to affected partitions. Prefect's dynamic task mapping facilitates this pattern, improving fault isolation and minimizing recomputation.

Example: Implementing an Idempotent ETL Task

Consider an extract-transform-load (ETL) task that writes processed batch data to a database table. A naive implementation risks duplicate inserts on retries or failures. An idempotent design employs the following principles:

```
from prefect import task
import hashlib

@task(retries=3, retry_delay_seconds=10)
def load_batch_to_db(batch_data):
    batch_id = hashlib.md5(str(batch_data).encode()).hexdigest()
    # Check if batch_id already exists in DB to avoid duplicates
    if not db_client.exists(batch_id):
        db_client.insert(batch_id, batch_data)
    else:
        print(f"Batch {batch_id} already loaded.")
```

This task calculates a deterministic batch identifier and queries the database to verify prior processing before insertion. The retry decorator ensures transient errors trigger automatic re-execution. The idempotence strategy allows this task to be safely retried without corrupting data integrity.

Integrating Prefect's Task and Flow States

Prefect's state model enriches error handling with fine-grained control:

- Upon failure, a task transitions to a `Failed` state, triggering any registered failure hooks.

- When retries are configured, the task moves to a `Retrying` state before re-execution.

- Timeout events transition tasks to a `TimedOut` state.

- Users may define custom states to encode domain-specific failure or compensation semantics.

Control flow within a Prefect flow can be made conditional on these states using built-in tasks such as case or custom control logic, enabling sophisticated recovery workflows.

Summary of Tools and Techniques

Prefect's architecture facilitates idempotence and fault tolerance through:

- **Declarative retries** with exponential backoff.

- **State handlers** that enable checkpointing and custom state transitions.

- **Failure hooks** enabling extensible response patterns to errors.

- **Result persistence** to external stores for resumption.

- **Mapping** and granularity control for partitioned processing.

- **Built-in timeout and cancel mechanisms** protecting against hung tasks.

By mastering these patterns and tools, engineers can architect workflows that withstand error conditions gracefully and support safe, repeatable execution essential to modern data engineering and automation pipelines.

4.2. High-Availability and Disaster Recovery Strategies

High-availability (HA) and disaster recovery (DR) in Prefect deployments advance beyond basic reliability by incorporating redundancy, failover mechanisms, and continuous workflow orchestration to minimize downtime. These strategies are essential to ensuring operational continuity and resilience during system disruptions, network failures, or infrastructure incidents.

Central to HA in Prefect is the deployment of a resilient orchestration infrastructure that avoids single points of failure. Prefect's architecture supports distributed execution with a decoupled control plane, enabling multiple orchestration nodes to coordinate task scheduling and state management. To achieve redundancy, multiple Prefect server or Prefect Orion API instances can be deployed behind a load balancer. This not only distributes workload but also facilitates failover by rerouting client requests to healthy nodes when individual components become unresponsive.

Workflow state persistence is critical to recovery and continuity. Prefect's state handlers and result backends (such as PostgreSQL or other robust databases) must be deployed with replication enabled. Replicated databases provide consistent, durable storage of task states and metadata across multiple nodes or regions, preventing data loss during node failures. Leveraging features like PostgreSQL's streaming replication or managed cloud databases with automated backups ensures that both task progress and logs survive transient failures or catastrophic infrastructure events.

Failover orchestration requires comprehensive health monitoring and automated recovery processes. System health can be monitored using heartbeat signals from agents and orchestration instances, linked to external alerting and remediation tools. When a failure is detected, automated scripts or orchestrator triggers replace the failed component, migrate running tasks, or restart affected flows. Prefect's flexible API enables integration with infrastructure-as-code tools, container orchestrators (e.g., Kubernetes), and CI/CD pipelines, thus facilitating timely recovery and minimizing manual intervention.

Minimizing downtime also depends on robust task and flow design. Flows should be idempotent, allowing safe retries and restarts without side effects. Checkpointing strategies can be implemented through state persistence features, enabling partial flow re-execution after failure instead of restarting entire workflows. Additionally, task timeouts and heartbeats can detect stalled executions, triggering recovery handlers to retry or escalate failures.

A practical example of HA in a Prefect deployment involves a multi-zone Kubernetes cluster running Prefect agents as pods with horizontal pod autoscaling. Agents in different availability zones connect to a Postgres database with cross-region replication. Load balancing layers distribute requests to multiple Prefect Orion APIs deployed as Kubernetes services configured with rolling updates, allowing seamless upgrades and failover. System health metrics are aggregated into Prometheus and Grafana, with alertmanager configured to trigger remediation workflows.

Disaster recovery plans complement HA by addressing scenarios where entire clusters or data centers become unavailable. Backup strategies must include regular snapshots of databases and file-based state stores, stored in geographically dispersed locations. Recovery workflows can be encoded as Prefect flows themselves, orchestrating complex procedures such as database restoration, infrastructure provisioning, and reinitialization of task schedulers.

Incorporating multi-cloud or hybrid-cloud strategies further enhances disaster resilience by avoiding vendor lock-in and providing fallback environments. Prefect flows can be configured with multiple execution environments, enabling workflows to migrate to alternate cloud providers transparently in case of regional outages.

Best practices for HA and DR in Prefect deployments include:

- **Redundant Orchestration Services**: Deploying multiple orchestrators with load balancing and failover support.

- **Durable State Storage**: Utilizing replicated databases and persistent storage with automated backups.

- **Monitoring and Alerts**: Implementing comprehensive health checks, heartbeat monitoring, and automated remediation mechanisms.

- **Idempotent Workflow Design**: Ensuring tasks and flows can be safely retried or resumed without unintended side effects.

- **Checkpointing and Partial Re-execution**: Leveraging Prefect state handlers to resume workflows at failure points.

- **Disaster Recovery Automation**: Encoding recovery procedures as Prefect flows to automate complex restoration processes.

- **Geographic and Cloud Diversity**: Architecting deployments across availability zones, regions, or providers for fault isolation.

Advanced Prefect deployments may combine these strategies with container orchestration platforms like Kubernetes to facilitate self-healing cluster behaviors, seamless service scaling, and declarative infrastructure management. Multi-region database clusters and cross-data center replication maintain state consistency and enable near-real-time recovery. Automated failover scripts or Prefect flows can be triggered by health events logged via Prometheus or cloud-native monitoring tools.

The orchestration layer itself can be designed for multi-tenancy and role-based access control, minimizing human error during recovery interventions and ensuring secure operations. Integration with infrastructure provisioning tools such as Terraform or Pulumi further enables consistent environment replication during disaster scenarios.

Prefect's modular design allows for flexible implementation of HA and DR tailored to organizational requirements and risk profiles. The deployment topology and recovery workflows can evolve iteratively as the scale and criticality of data pipelines increase. Ultimately, combining robust infrastructure, observability, automated orchestration, and best-practice workflows results in resilient pipeline execution environments that maintain business continuity even in the face of failures and disasters.

4.3. Scaling Agents, Tasks, and Workflows

Scaling Prefect deployments effectively requires a nuanced application of both horizontal and vertical strategies, designed to optimize resource utilization while maintaining operational reliability across diverse workload demands. Prefect's architecture, centered around its agents, tasks, and flows, provides intrinsic flexibility that can be leveraged to handle increasing scale within data orchestration environments.

Horizontal scaling primarily focuses on increasing the number of Prefect agents to distribute workload execution across multiple compute resources. Each agent acts as a worker polling the Prefect API for flow run assignments. By deploying additional agents-whether as containerized instances, virtual machines, or ephemeral serverless functions-organizations can parallelize workload consumption, mitigate bottlenecks, and improve fault tolerance. Dynamic agent provisioning is central in this approach; agents may be scheduled to scale up or down automatically using infrastructure-as-code tools or orchestration platforms such as Kubernetes, AWS ECS, or Azure Container Instances. This elasticity ensures that agent availability closely matches real-time demand, thereby optimizing cost and performance.

For example, configuring Prefect agents in a Kubernetes cluster can be achieved by defining a Kubernetes Deployment with an appropriate autoscaler, such as the Horizontal Pod Autoscaler (HPA). The HPA can monitor CPU or memory utilization or even custom Prometheus metrics corresponding to agent queue lengths to trigger scaling events. Each newly spawned pod contains a Prefect agent instance capable of handling flow runs, supporting a virtually unbounded horizontal scaling model limited only by cluster capacity and API rate limits.

Vertical scaling complements this by enhancing the compute capacity and parallel processing proficiency of individual agents and their hosted execution environments. Prefect tasks, executed as discrete units of work within flows, often benefit from additional CPU cores, increased memory, or specialized hardware (like GPUs) in vertical scaling scenarios. Vertical scaling is particularly advantageous when tasks are CPU-intensive, memory-bound, or require optimized data locality to reduce latency. For instance, configuring an agent's runtime environment with higher resource quotas or deploying it on high-performance virtual machines enables individual flows with resource-heavy tasks to execute more efficiently.

The orchestration of tasks at scale involves distributing the task executions across a pool of available resources while preserving task dependencies and execution order within flows. Prefect leverages dynamic task scheduling and asynchronous execution models, which allow for parallel task evaluation and concurrent processing to maximize throughput. Within large environments, task-level concurrency hinges on the executor configuration; for example, using Prefect's Dask executor enables scaling out task execution to a distributed Dask cluster. By integrating Prefect with Dask, tasks submit futures to the cluster's scheduler, which manages execution on available compute workers. This integration provides resilience and scalability since the cluster can dynamically add or remove workers based on workload, effectively balancing tasks across multiple machines.

At the workflow orchestration layer, managing many flows concurrently becomes a distinct challenge as deployments grow in complexity and scale. Prefect's centralized orchestration server and API must handle increased flow run creation, monitoring, and state transitions effectively. Techniques to support high concurrency include sharding flow queues or segregating flows by project or team, thereby distributing the workload for the orchestration backend. This approach reduces contention and speeds up flow assignment to agents. Moreover, leveraging Prefect's Cloud or Prefect Server with autoscaled database and API backend components ensures that the orchestration infrastructure remains responsive.

Scaling across multiple queues can be accomplished by categorizing flows into distinct queues, each served by specialized agents. This segmentation allows prioritization and resource allocation tailored to specific workflow requirements, such as isolating high-priority production flows from development or testing workloads. Agents can be configured to listen to one or more queues, directing execution capacity where it is most needed. Combined with dynamic agent scaling, this queue-based design fosters granular control of flow execution concurrency at scale.

An additional technique is implementing rate limiting and retry policies within tasks and flows to manage transient resource contention or external system load limits. When scaling horizontally and vertically, distributed tasks might compete for database connections, APIs, or storage I/O. Applying intelligent backoff and throttling policies reduces errors and improves overall throughput in large, distributed Prefect deployments.

Scaling Prefect deployments requires an orchestrated strategy utilizing dynamic provisioning of agents to parallelize execution horizontally, augmenting compute resources vertically to enhance task performance, and supporting numerous concurrent flows through queue segmentation and backend scalability. The integration of autoscaling mechanisms with orchestrator configuration and execution environment tuning enables organizations to maintain robust, cost-effective orchestration platforms tailored to evolving operational demands and workflow complexities.

4.4. Throughput Optimization and Bottleneck Analysis

Performance optimization in Prefect pipelines hinges on the precise identification, diagnosis, and resolution of bottlenecks that impede throughput and increase latency. In distributed workflow orchestration, execution inefficiencies stem from various factors including resource contention, suboptimal task parallelism, or external system dependencies. This section dissects practical methods and tools to profile pipeline executions rigorously, and demonstrates how targeted interventions can significantly enhance performance for critical workloads.

Profiling involves systematic measurement of task execution times, resource utilizations, and data transfer latencies within a pipeline. Prefect's instrumentation capabilities allow collection of detailed metadata about each flow run and task execution through its telemetry and logging frameworks. Exporting this runtime data to external monitoring solutions, such as Prometheus or cloud-native observability platforms, enables comprehensive analysis over time.

At the core of throughput analysis is the identification of tasks with disproportionate execution durations relative to their expected cost or criticality within the dependency graph. Prefect's task state transitions and event hooks can be employed to capture timestamps when each task moves from queued to running, and subsequently to completion or failure. This temporal data, visualized using time-series tools or custom dashboards, exposes chokepoints where pipeline progress is impeded.

For example, a typical profiling snippet involves attaching state handlers to log task durations:

```
from prefect import task, Flow
from prefect.engine.state import Success

def log_task_duration(task, old_state, new_state):
```

```
if isinstance(new_state, Success):
    duration = new_state.timestamp - old_state.timestamp
    logger.info(f"Task {task.name} completed in {duration.
 total_seconds()} seconds")
 return new_state

@task(state_handlers=[log_task_duration])
def example_task():
    # task implementation
    pass

with Flow("example") as flow:
    example_task()
```

The aggregated logs facilitate subsequent bottleneck identification by highlighting tasks that consistently exhibit high latency or variance.

Bottlenecks fall broadly into categories involving I/O delays, CPU-bound computations, and communication overhead. In data-centric workflows, common sources include slow database queries or external API calls that serialize task execution. Similarly, task dependencies that force sequential execution can diminish parallel throughput opportunities.

To exemplify, consider a pipeline stage reliant on a slow external API. If multiple downstream tasks are contingent upon this stage, its latency cascades through the pipeline. Prefect's dynamic mapping features help expose such situations by enabling parallelization over iterable inputs, but only when upstream tasks are non-blocking.

Resource saturation is another critical bottleneck, often occurring in on-premises or self-hosted agents where CPU, memory, or network bandwidth limits are reached. Monitoring system-level metrics alongside Prefect task metrics aids in associating pipeline slowdown with resource exhaustion, guiding decisions for horizontal scaling or hardware upgrades.

The Prefect UI provides an immediate overview of flow run behavior, illustrating task durations and dependencies graphically. The timeline and flow map views allow drill-down into problematic tasks. Augmenting this visual analysis with programmatic queries via Prefect's API supports automated detection of anomalies or regressions in performance.

A practical diagnostic approach involves scripting flow run comparisons, isolating tasks whose running times exceed historical baselines or SLA thresholds:

```
from prefect.client import Client
import statistics

client = Client()

def slow_tasks(flow_run_id, threshold_seconds):
    flow_run = client.get_flow_run_info(flow_run_id)
    task_runs = client.list_task_runs(flow_run_id=flow_run_id)
    slow = []
    for tr in task_runs:
        duration = (tr.state.timestamp - tr.state.cached_inputs.
    get('start_time')) \
                    .total_seconds() if tr.state and tr.state.
    timestamp else None
        if duration and duration > threshold_seconds:
            slow.append((tr.task_name, duration))
    return slow
```

Combining such scripts with automated alerting mechanisms ensures proactive response to emerging bottlenecks.

Effective remediation requires understanding task characteristics and pipeline topology. Parallelism is a primary lever-Prefect's infrastructure enables concurrent task execution if dependencies allow. Where inherently sequential dependencies exist, micro-optimizations such as asynchronous I/O, caching intermediate results, or batching can reduce wait times.

Task retries and failures also affect throughput. Configuring back-off strategies, timeouts, and failure policies in Prefect tasks reduces cascading delays. For compute-heavy tasks, offloading intensive operations to specialized hardware or distributed compute clusters, integrated through Prefect agents, improves overall pipeline responsiveness.

Prefect's ability to partition workloads via dynamic mapping and subflows can break monolithic tasks into smaller units, allowing finer-grained scheduling and improved utilization of available resources. This modularization also facilitates incremental performance tuning, isolating hotspots with greater precision.

As an example, converting a serial batch processing task into a parallel mapped task reduces end-to-end latency:

```
@task
def process_item(item):
    # expensive computation
    pass

with Flow("batch_processing") as flow:
    items = [1, 2, 3, 4, 5]
    results = process_item.map(items)
```

Ensuring sufficient concurrency settings and agent capacity completes the throughput enhancement.

A real-world demonstration involves a data ingestion pipeline exhibiting prolonged task durations due to external database query slowness and sequential dependency chains. Profiling revealed specific extraction tasks occupying over 70% of total execution time. Introducing connection pooling improved external database response rates, while restructuring the pipeline to process multiple partitions in parallel leveraged Prefect's dynamic mapping to reduce end-to-end latency by 45%.

By integrating granular telemetry and iterative tuning-adjusting task concurrency limits, caching intermediate artifacts, and tuning agent configurations-the pipeline achieved stable throughput under increased load, evidencing the value of systematic bottleneck analysis.

- Leverage Prefect's built-in instrumentation and external monitoring systems for continuous profiling.

- Identify tasks with disproportionate execution times or resource demands through aggregated logs and API queries.

- Exploit dynamic mapping, parallelism, and subflows to maximize utilization of compute resources.

- Address external I/O bottlenecks via caching, connection pooling, or asynchronous calls.

- Continuously monitor system metrics to correlate resource saturation with pipeline performance.

- Employ strict failure handling and retry mechanisms to prevent cascading delays.

Applying these strategies fosters robust pipeline designs capable of sustaining high throughput and minimizing latency in demanding workloads.

4.5. Advanced Caching and Checkpointing Mechanisms

The effective management of intermediate results and fault tolerance in complex distributed workflows relies heavily on advanced caching and checkpointing strategies. These mechanisms not only accelerate repeated execution through intelligent reuse of prior computations but also significantly improve robustness by enabling fast recovery from partial failures and interruptions.

Distributed caching involves storing intermediate results or artifacts in a shared, often networked, storage system accessible across the distributed environment. This approach contrasts with local caching, which confines stored data to a single execution node. By leveraging distributed caching, workflows gain the ability to recognize previously computed outcomes, thereby avoiding redundant processing and reducing total runtime in iterative and parameterized runs.

A common design pattern is the content-addressable cache, where cache keys are generated deterministically based on the task inputs, environment context, and code versions. Prefect's caching mechanism embodies this principle through configurable cache keys that incorporate these elements, ensuring cache validity: if any input or code changes, the corresponding key shifts and the cache is invalidated for that execution. This deterministic approach facilitates cache hits with high precision, fostering cache reuse even across distributed and parallel executions.

Prefect extends caching capabilities through hyperparameters controlling caching behavior at the task or flow level. For instance, the `cache_for` parameter can specify time intervals to declare cache validity, balancing aggressive caching with the need for fresh computations when required. Additionally, the `cache_validator` can implement custom logic for cache validation, such as hashing strategies or external status checks, offering fine-grained control over cache retention policies.

Checkpointing complements caching by persistently saving the internal state of a workflow or its constituent tasks at defined execution points. This persistence enables workflows to resume from the latest checkpoint following interruptions such as hardware failures, network partitions, or unexpected terminations. Effective checkpointing must address consistency, durability, and minimal performance overhead. Distributed systems typically store checkpoints in reliable object stores or distributed file systems (e.g., S3, HDFS) that are fault-tolerant and highly available.

From a design perspective, idempotent task definitions are essential to maximize the benefits of checkpointing. When tasks can be safely retried and resumed without side effects, checkpointing mechanisms can selectively rerun only failed or unfinished components rather than restarting entire workflows. Combined with Prefect's state handlers and retry logic, checkpointing integrates seamlessly into robust, fault-tolerant pipelines.

Prefect offers built-in checkpointing features via its state handlers and result storage configuration. Tasks can be linked to result storage backends where outputs and metadata are serialized to persistent stores automatically. During execution recovery, Prefect interrogates these results to restore prior outputs and states, effectively resuming the workflow mid-execution. The modularity of Prefect's result storage allows integration with various backends, including cloud storage solutions and databases, matching organization-specific infrastructural requirements.

To illustrate these concepts, consider the following example configuration for a Prefect task that uses caching with a one-day expiration and persistent result storage to S3:

```
from prefect import task
from prefect.engine.results import S3Result
from prefect.tasks.prefect import StartFlowRun
import datetime

@task(cache_for=datetime.timedelta(days=1),
      result=S3Result(bucket='my-prefect-results'),
      checkpoint=True)
def expensive_computation(x: int) -> int:
    # Computationally intensive logic here
    return x * x
```

In this setup, the task output is cached for 24 hours. The checkpoint=True flag ensures the task result is saved to the specified S3 bucket. Upon re-execution within the cache window, Prefect will retrieve the output from the cache instead of recomputing it. If the workflow is interrupted, the checkpoint allows resuming from the last successful state without re-executing already completed tasks.

Advanced strategies can also use hierarchical or multi-tier caching, where an initial local cache acts as a first-level cache providing rapid access, while distributed caches serve as a fallback. This pattern combines low latency and high availability. Additionally, selective or partial checkpointing can optimize performance by saving only states of critical path tasks or significant intermediate data points rather than the entire computation graph.

An emerging practice is to couple caching and checkpointing

with workflow snapshotting, where the entire workflow's execution graph, including states and results, is serialized at runtime milestones. This snapshotting facilitates reproducibility, debugging, and audit trails by capturing the exact execution context.

In high-concurrency environments, cache and checkpoint consistency must be managed carefully to avoid race conditions or stale data usage. Prefect's orchestration engine handles such concurrency concerns by enforcing state transitions atomically, combined with external transactional storage guarantees when supported.

Overall, the synergy of distributed caching and checkpointing addresses two primary challenges in modern cloud-native workflows: minimizing redundant computations and providing robust failure recovery. By incorporating content-addressable cache keys, configurable cache expiration, persistent result storage, and idempotent task design, Prefect enables highly efficient, resilient pipelines capable of operating at scale with minimal human intervention.

4.6. Handling Non-deterministic or Unreliable Tasks

Workflows operating in real-world environments frequently encounter non-deterministic behavior, intermittent failures, and flaky external dependencies. Such uncertainty can degrade overall system reliability, reduce throughput, and impair user experience. Building confidence into these workflows requires deliberate strategies to manage unpredictability by detecting, isolating, and mitigating failure modes without sacrificing efficiency or maintainability.

One fundamental approach involves implementing *retry policies* with backoff and jitter. When a task fails due to transient reasons (e.g., network timeout, rate limiting, or temporary service unavailability), automatically retrying enables the workflow to recover without manual intervention. Employing exponential backoff reduces load on the system during high failure rates while randomized jitter avoids synchronized retries across many clients, which can cause cascading failures. For example, a basic retry policy can be conceptualized as

$$T_{n+1} = \min(T_{\max}, T_n \times 2) + \text{jitter}$$

where T_n is the wait time before the nth retry attempt, and $T_{\max}$ is a timeout ceiling.

However, blind retries can exacerbate systemic issues, so incorporating *circuit breakers* becomes critical to prevent wasteful attempts against unresponsive or malfunctioning services. Circuit breakers monitor failure rates and response times; when these exceed predefined thresholds, the breaker trips and halts further requests to the failing component for a cooldown period. This allows the system to recover or administrators to intervene. The classic state machine model of a circuit breaker includes three states: Closed (normal operation), Open (stop requests), and Half-Open (test if normal operation can resume).

To illustrate, a task interacting with an external API can be wrapped in a circuit breaker as follows (pseudocode):

```
class CircuitBreaker:
    def __init__(self, failure_threshold, recovery_timeout):
        self.fail_count = 0
        self.failure_threshold = failure_threshold
        self.recovery_timeout = recovery_timeout
        self.state = 'Closed'
        self.last_failure_time = None

    def call(self, func, *args, **kwargs):
        if self.state == 'Open':
            if time_since(self.last_failure_time) > self.
recovery_timeout:
                self.state = 'Half-Open'
            else:
                raise ServiceUnavailableError()

        try:
            result = func(*args, **kwargs)
```

```
        self._reset()
        if self.state == 'Half-Open':
            self.state = 'Closed'
        return result
    except Exception:
        self._record_failure()
        raise

def _record_failure(self):
    self.fail_count += 1
    self.last_failure_time = current_time()
    if self.fail_count >= self.failure_threshold:
        self.state = 'Open'

def _reset(self):
    self.fail_count = 0
    self.last_failure_time = None
```

Next, *idempotency* is a key concept to ensure repeated executions of the same task do not have unintended side effects. This is especially pertinent when retries or parallel speculative executions are employed. Each task implementation must be designed or augmented to handle repeated inputs gracefully, either by detecting duplicate operations through unique request identifiers or by ensuring modifications are atomic and state-aware.

Implementing *fallback mechanisms* further enhances resilience. When a primary resource is unavailable or produces unreliable results, workflows should degrade gracefully by switching to secondary data sources, cached values, or simplified computations that maintain partial functionality. These fallbacks can be invoked dynamically based on health-check signals or service quality metrics.

Monitoring and observability are indispensable for identifying non-deterministic behaviors and informing automatic recovery policies. Effective workflows incorporate comprehensive telemetry on task success rates, latency distributions, error classes, and resource utilization. Alerts triggered by anomaly detection can prompt human attention or automatically adjust retry and circuit-breaker parameters.

To manage flaky external components, *task timeouts* must be enforced strictly to avoid cascading delays. Imposing upper bounds on execution time allows the workflow engine to reclaim resources and proceed with contingency plans if a task stalls. Timeouts combined with retries and circuit breakers create composable safeguards against various failure modes.

Consider an example combining these strategies in a network request task:

```
def robust_network_call(request, circuit_breaker):
    max_attempts = 5
    base_delay = 0.5  # seconds

    for attempt in range(1, max_attempts + 1):
        try:
            return circuit_breaker.call(send_request, request,
        timeout=2)
        except ServiceUnavailableError:
            raise   # Circuit breaker open, abort immediately
        except TimeoutError:
            if attempt == max_attempts:
                raise
        except TransientNetworkError:
            if attempt == max_attempts:
                raise

        delay = base_delay * (2 ** (attempt - 1)) + random.
    uniform(0, 0.1)
        time.sleep(delay)

    # Optional fallback if all attempts fail
    return fetch_cached_response(request)
```

In distributed and parallel workflows, *compensation or rollback actions* are essential to handle partial failures. When certain tasks succeed while others fail, explicitly reversing or compensating for completed operations ensures consistent end states. Compensation logic relies on well-defined task boundaries and persistent tracking of each step's outcome.

Moreover, maintaining *eventual consistency* in workflows affected by non-deterministic external factors is a practical tradeoff. Acknowledging that perfect atomicity is not achievable under unreliability allows design patterns such as event sourcing and state reconciliation to restore system coherence asynchronously.

Finally, leveraging *workflow orchestration frameworks* that embed native support for retries, timeouts, circuit breakers, and compensation simplifies implementing these robustness strategies. Such platforms often provide declarative specifications allowing dynamic adaptation to failure modes without extensive custom code, aligning operational flexibility with deterministic workflow logic.

Integrating all these mechanisms produces workflows that anticipate and gracefully navigate uncertainty. The key lies in embracing uncertainty as an inherent characteristic of real-world systems, architecting workflows with defensive programming paradigms, layered fault tolerance, and observable feedback loops. Only then can complex pipelines deliver reliable and predictable outcomes despite the intrinsically non-deterministic or unreliable nature of their components.

Chapter 5

Integrating Prefect with the Data & DevOps Ecosystem

Prefect doesn't just orchestrate workflows—it connects the dots across the entire data and DevOps landscape. This chapter reveals how Prefect fits seamlessly into a world of diverse data stores, APIs, automation pipelines, and cloud-native technologies, empowering you to unlock new synergies and accelerate your end-to-end engineering workflows.

5.1. Database, Filesystem, and Cloud Storage Integrations

Prefect's flexible architecture and extensive adapter ecosystem enable seamless interaction with diverse data sources and sinks, encompassing relational and NoSQL databases, local and distributed filesystems, as well as cloud storage services. This section examines integration patterns that demonstrate how Prefect workflows can orchestrate complex data pipelines by programmatically reading, writing, and managing data across these storage backends.

Relational Database Integration

Relational databases remain core components in most data ecosystems, offering structured schema, ACID compliance, and powerful query capabilities. Prefect's `SqlAlchemyConnector` and native task libraries facilitate connection management and SQL execution within flows. A canonical integration involves extracting data for transformation or loading processed results back into the database.

For example, connecting to a PostgreSQL database and executing a query within a Prefect flow can be structured as follows:

```
from prefect import task, flow
from prefect_sqlalchemy import SqlAlchemyConnector

@task
def fetch_data(connector: SqlAlchemyConnector, query: str):
    with connector.get_connection(begin=False) as conn:
        result = conn.execute(query)
        return result.fetchall()

@flow
def etl_postgres_flow():
    connector = SqlAlchemyConnector(connection_url="postgresql+
    psycopg2://user:pass@localhost/dbname")
    data = fetch_data(connector, "SELECT * FROM users WHERE
    active = TRUE;")
    # Further processing steps here
```

This pattern emphasizes abstraction of connection handling via connectors, enabling reuse and central management of database credentials and connection parameters. Prefect's caching and retry policies can further enhance robustness against transient failures.

Writing data back to a relational store often leverages bulk insert commands or ORM frameworks. Prefect tasks wrapping SQLAlchemy sessions can perform inserts, updates, or merges, ensuring transactional integrity within orchestrated workflows.

NoSQL Database Connectivity

NoSQL databases such as MongoDB, Cassandra, and Redis provide scalable, schema-flexible alternatives for certain applications. Prefect integrates with these services typically through community or official clients wrapped in tasks. For instance, a MongoDB task might perform document retrieval or update operations asynchronously.

The following outlines a pattern for querying a MongoDB collection:

```
from prefect import task, flow
from pymongo import MongoClient

@task
def query_mongo(uri: str, db_name: str, collection_name: str,
    filter_query: dict):
    client = MongoClient(uri)
    collection = client[db_name][collection_name]
    documents = list(collection.find(filter_query))
    client.close()
    return documents

@flow
def mongo_data_flow():
    docs = query_mongo(
        uri="mongodb://user:pass@host:27017",
        db_name="analytics",
        collection_name="events",
        filter_query={"event_type": "click"}
    )
    # Process documents
```

Similar patterns apply to other NoSQL technologies, with Prefect's task abstraction facilitating parameterization, result caching, and integration with downstream processing operators.

Filesystem Interaction Patterns

Accessing data from local or distributed filesystems is a fundamental operation in many workflows. Prefect provides native tasks and API utilities to work with filesystems abstracted by URI schemes, including POSIX paths, NFS mounts, HDFS, or cloud storage via respective mounted volumes.

File reading and writing tasks can be composed to facilitate ETL operations or checkpointing intermediate results. A typical pattern to read a CSV file, transform it, and write out the results is:

```
import pandas as pd
from prefect import task, flow
import pathlib


@task
def read_csv(path: str) -> pd.DataFrame:
    return pd.read_csv(path)


@task
def transform_data(df: pd.DataFrame) -> pd.DataFrame:
    # Example transformation
    df["processed_flag"] = True
    return df


@task
def write_csv(df: pd.DataFrame, output_path: str):
    df.to_csv(output_path, index=False)


@flow
def fs_etl_flow():
    input_path = "/mnt/data/input/events.csv"
    output_path = "/mnt/data/output/events_clean.csv"
    df = read_csv(input_path)
    df_transformed = transform_data(df)
    write_csv(df_transformed, output_path)
```

Beyond local filesystems, Prefect can orchestrate interactions with HDFS or object-store-mounted volumes by updating paths accordingly, often leveraging existing Python client libraries within tasks.

Cloud Storage Services

Modern data workflows increasingly leverage cloud storage solutions such as Amazon S3, Google Cloud Storage, Azure Blob Storage, and others. Prefect integrates with these platforms via provider-specific SDKs or through its rich task libraries, enabling robust, scalable interactions with bucket-based object stores.

A common orchestration pattern is downloading raw data objects, processing them locally or in distributed compute, and then uploading results back to a cloud storage location. For example, to download and upload files from S3:

```
from prefect_aws import AwsCredentials
from prefect_aws.s3 import S3Download, S3Upload
from prefect import flow

@flow
def s3_workflow(bucket: str, key_in: str, key_out: str):
    aws_creds = AwsCredentials()  # Assumes credentials
    configured in environment
    local_file = S3Download(bucket=bucket, aws_credentials=
    aws_creds)(key_in)
    # Perform processing on local_file here
    S3Upload(bucket=bucket, aws_credentials=aws_creds)(path=
    local_file, key=key_out)
```

Prefect's modular design permits chaining these tasks and handling large datasets efficiently. It also supports glob-style path expansions and streaming operations when interacting with cloud storage objects, reducing memory footprints during execution.

Managing Credentials and Security

Secure management of credentials is paramount when integrating with databases and cloud storages. Prefect's `Secrets` and `Blocks` abstractions provide secure storage and injection of sensitive configuration details such as connection strings, API keys, or certificates.

Encapsulating credentials within reusable blocks decouples secret management from flow logic, enabling safer deployment pipelines. For example:

```
from prefect import flow
from prefect.blocks.system import Secret

@flow
def secure_db_flow():
    secret_block = Secret.load("prod-db-connection-string")
    conn_string = secret_block.get()
    # Utilize conn_string in database connector
```

This practice ensures credentials never appear in code repositories or logs, aligning with industry best practices.

Data Management Considerations

When orchestrating file and database operations, managing idempotency and data consistency is essential. Prefect's built-in state handlers, caching, and checkpointing features allow workflows to detect data presence to avoid redundant processing or partial writes.

Workflow designers often implement existence checks or timestamp comparisons as predicates within tasks to prevent overwriting valuable historical data, enabling robust incremental data pipelines.

```
@task
def check_data_exists(bucket: str, key: str) -> bool:
    # Logic to check if S3 object exists
    pass

@flow
def conditional_upload_flow():
    if not check_data_exists("my-bucket", "output/processed.json
    "):
        # Perform upload task
```

Combining these patterns with Prefect's retry policies and concurrency controls fosters resilient data pipelines across heterogeneous storage platforms.

5.2. API, HTTP, and Message Queue Orchestration

Orchestrating external services within modern data workflows often requires seamless integration with REST APIs, HTTP endpoints, and message brokers such as Kafka or RabbitMQ. Prefect, as a flexible workflow orchestration tool, excels in connecting and managing these diverse components to facilitate robust service choreography, handle asynchronous operations, and enable streaming data processing.

Prefect's integration with HTTP services leverages Python's extensive HTTP client libraries such as `requests` or `httpx`, providing both synchronous and asynchronous interaction capabilities. Tasks designed to invoke REST APIs commonly follow a pattern encapsulating connectivity, authentication, request dispatching, and response handling.

A typical synchronous API call task may take the form:

```python
import requests
from prefect import task, Flow

@task
def fetch_data_from_api(url: str, headers: dict = None):
    response = requests.get(url, headers=headers)
    response.raise_for_status()
    return response.json()

with Flow("api_call_example") as flow:
    data = fetch_data_from_api("https://api.example.com/data")
```

This structure ensures robust error handling via `raise_for_status()`, which Prefect captures to mark task failure, enabling dynamic retries or alternative branching. For APIs supporting asynchronous clients, `httpx` or `aiohttp` may be employed:

```python
import httpx
from prefect import task

@task
async def fetch_data_async(url: str):
    async with httpx.AsyncClient() as client:
        response = await client.get(url)
        response.raise_for_status()
        return response.json()
```

Utilizing asynchronous tasks is particularly advantageous when multiple independent API calls can be executed concurrently, reducing end-to-end workflow latency.

Asynchronous orchestration in Prefect is crucial when interacting with APIs exhibiting varying latencies or when polling is required for resource readiness. Prefect supports the concept of asynchronous tasks and the extensible architecture permits combining event-driven and time-based triggers.

For example, consider orchestrating a workflow that initiates a long-running external process via a POST API call and subsequently polls an HTTP endpoint for completion status. This can be implemented using a loop with retry or wait mechanisms:

```python
from prefect import task, Flow
import time
from datetime import timedelta
import requests
import prefect


@task
def initiate_process(api_url: str) -> str:
    response = requests.post(api_url)
    response.raise_for_status()
    return response.json()['process_id']

@task(max_retries=10, retry_delay=timedelta(seconds=30))
def check_status(api_url: str, process_id: str) -> bool:
    response = requests.get(f"{api_url}/{process_id}/status")
    response.raise_for_status()
    status = response.json()['status']
    if status == "completed":
        return True
    elif status == "failed":
        raise ValueError("Process failed")
    else:
        raise prefect.engine.signals.RETRY()

with Flow("async_api_polling") as flow:
    pid = initiate_process("https://api.example.com/start")
    done = check_status("https://api.example.com/process", pid)
```

This pattern utilizes Prefect's retry mechanism to implement asynchronous polling transparently, avoiding resource blocking and effectively managing service readiness checks.

Message brokers such as Kafka and RabbitMQ serve as pivotal middleware in distributed architectures, enabling decoupled communication, streaming data ingestion, and event-driven processing patterns. Prefect's capability to interface with these brokers facilitates complex orchestration workflows that react to real-time streams and message events.

Integration with Kafka

Apache Kafka orchestrations typically require producing messages to topics and consuming streams for downstream processing. Prefect tasks can leverage popular Python Kafka clients like `confluent-kafka` or `kafka-python`.

A producer pattern task might resemble:

```
from confluent_kafka import Producer
from prefect import task

@task
def kafka_produce(topic: str, message: bytes, conf: dict):
    producer = Producer(conf)
    producer.produce(topic, message)
    producer.flush()
```

For Kafka consumers, challenges arise due to indefinite streaming. Prefect can control consumption by defining tasks that poll within a timeout or batch window, returning collected messages for subsequent processing:

```
from confluent_kafka import Consumer, KafkaError
from prefect import task

@task
def kafka_consume(topic: str, conf: dict, max_msgs: int = 100):
    consumer = Consumer(conf)
    consumer.subscribe([topic])
    messages = []
    while len(messages) < max_msgs:
        msg = consumer.poll(1.0)
        if msg is None:
            continue
        if msg.error():
            if msg.error().code() == KafkaError._PARTITION_EOF:
                break
            else:
                raise Exception(msg.error())
        messages.append(msg.value())
    consumer.close()
    return messages
```

These collected message batches then become natural inputs to downstream Prefect tasks, enabling event-driven or micro-batch processing architectures.

Integration with RabbitMQ

RabbitMQ's AMQP protocol necessitates client libraries such as pika for interfacing. Producing and consuming messages within Prefect tasks follows analogous principles, with emphasis on connection management and message acknowledgment semantics:

```
import pika
from prefect import task


@task
def rabbitmq_publish(queue_name: str, message: bytes,
    connection_params):
    connection = pika.BlockingConnection(pika.
    ConnectionParameters(**connection_params))
    channel = connection.channel()
    channel.queue_declare(queue=queue_name)
    channel.basic_publish(exchange='',
                          routing_key=queue_name,
                          body=message)
    connection.close()


@task
def rabbitmq_consume(queue_name: str, connection_params, max_msgs
    : int = 10):
    connection = pika.BlockingConnection(pika.
    ConnectionParameters(**connection_params))
    channel = connection.channel()
    channel.queue_declare(queue=queue_name)

    messages = []

    def callback(ch, method, properties, body):
        messages.append(body)
        ch.basic_ack(delivery_tag=method.delivery_tag)
        if len(messages) >= max_msgs:
            ch.stop_consuming()

    channel.basic_consume(queue=queue_name, on_message_callback=
    callback)
    channel.start_consuming()
    connection.close()
    return messages
```

Handling message acknowledgments and flow control during consumption is essential to maintain reliability and avoid message loss or duplication.

Orchestration leveraging APIs and messaging systems often involves composing multiple independent services into a cohesive workflow with complex interactions. Prefect supports this choreography through task dependencies, triggers, and mapped tasks. Key patterns include:

- *Fan-out/Fan-in*: Parallelize requests or message publishing across multiple endpoints or topics, then aggregate results using mapped tasks and upstream joins.

- *Event-based triggers*: Use message consumption tasks to conditionally trigger subsequent tasks or flows, enabling reactive orchestration based on real-time events.

- *Circuit breakers and dead-letter processing*: Implement fault tolerance by catching exceptions from external calls or broker failures, routing problematic messages or requests to alternative paths for inspection or retries.

An example of service choreography with API calls and message queues may resemble the following conceptual flow:

- Initiate data extraction via a REST API.

- Publish extracted data chunks asynchronously to Kafka topics.

- Consume messages from Kafka into parallel processing tasks.

- Aggregate processed results and notify via HTTP callbacks.

Such integration patterns ensure scalability, resiliency, and observability by leveraging Prefect's orchestration semantics combined with external service capabilities.

Mastering orchestration between Prefect, HTTP-based services, and messaging systems involves combining synchronous and asynchronous API interactions, streaming data processing via message brokers, and comprehensive error handling strategies. Adhering to clear separation of concerns-where API calls perform discrete operations, message brokers handle event sequencing, and Prefect coordinates flow execution-yields maintainable, fault-tolerant distributed workflows capable of responding dynamically to external system states and high-throughput data streams.

5.3. Secrets Management and Credentials Injection

The protection of sensitive data and credentials is a fundamental concern in orchestrating secure and compliant workflows. Robust secrets management solutions provide centralized control, auditability, and dynamic access to credentials, ensuring that sensitive information is never hard-coded or exposed in plaintext. This section explores the integration of Prefect workflows with widely adopted secret management systems—HashiCorp Vault, AWS Secrets Manager—and Prefect's native secrets framework, highlighting best practices for injecting credentials securely into task executions.

HashiCorp Vault Integration

HashiCorp Vault is a popular open-source tool designed for securely storing and accessing secrets. Vault achieves this by encrypting secrets at rest and tightly controlling access via authentication policies and tokens.

Establishing Connectivity and Authentication To integrate Vault with Prefect, the workflow environment must have network access to the Vault server and suitable authentication credentials. Authentication methods include AppRole, Kubernetes auth, or token-based authentication. For example, with AppRole, Prefect agents can be configured with role IDs and secret IDs to authenticate and retrieve tokens dynamically.

Retrieving Secrets at Runtime Prefect tasks can interact with Vault via the Python client library hvac. Using environment variables or Prefect's secret handling mechanisms, tokens can be cached securely within task runtime contexts, allowing code snippets like the following to fetch database credentials:

```
import hvac

client = hvac.Client(url="https://vault.example.com", token="s.
    XYZ123")
secret_response = client.secrets.kv.v2.read_secret_version(path="
    database/creds")
db_username = secret_response['data']['data']['username']
db_password = secret_response['data']['data']['password']
```

This approach ensures that credentials are retrieved only when needed and are never stored in source code or logs.

Dynamic Secrets and Leasing Vault supports dynamic secrets generation, which allows Prefect workflows to obtain ephemeral credentials with limited TTLs, reducing the risk of long-lived credential leakage. Prefect can be orchestrated to renew these secrets or revoke them upon completion by embedding logic in flows to call Vault lease management APIs.

AWS Secrets Manager Integration

AWS Secrets Manager facilitates secure storage, automatic rotation, and fine-grained access control of secrets within the AWS ecosystem. Prefect workflows running in AWS or hybrid environments benefit from its direct integration capabilities.

Access Management via IAM Permissions to retrieve secrets from AWS Secrets Manager rely on IAM roles and policies. It is recommended to assign least privilege roles to Prefect agents or execution environments so that secrets access is restricted to necessary scopes.

Fetching Secrets in Prefect Tasks Prefect tasks can utilize Boto3, the AWS SDK for Python, to programmatically fetch secrets:

```
import boto3
import base64
from botocore.exceptions import ClientError

def get_secret(secret_name, region_name="us-west-2"):
    session = boto3.session.Session()
    client = session.client(service_name='secretsmanager',
     region_name=region_name)
    try:
        get_secret_value_response = client.get_secret_value(
        SecretId=secret_name)
    except ClientError as e:
        raise e

    if 'SecretString' in get_secret_value_response:
        return get_secret_value_response['SecretString']
    else:
        decoded_binary_secret = base64.b64decode(
     get_secret_value_response['SecretBinary'])
        return decoded_binary_secret
```

This function can be invoked within Prefect tasks to dynamically retrieve secrets at runtime, providing secure and auditable access to credentials.

Automatic Rotation and Versioning Leveraging AWS Secrets Manager's automatic rotation capabilities reduces operational burden and enhances security posture. Prefect workflows should be designed to gracefully handle credential changes by fetching secrets afresh when tasks execute, rather than caching sensitive values persistently.

Prefect Native Secrets Management

Prefect's native secrets management facilities offer a streamlined approach to managing sensitive information within Prefect Cloud or Prefect Server.

Defining and Utilizing Prefect Secrets Secrets can be created and stored via the Prefect UI or CLI, assigned a unique key, and associated with environment variables. These secrets are encrypted and stored securely within Prefect's backend systems.

When defining flows, Prefect's `prefect.client.Secret` class or environment variable interpolation enables secure injection of secrets without exposing values in logs or configuration files:

```
from prefect import task, Flow
from prefect.client import Secret

@task
def use_secret():
    api_key = Secret("MY_API_KEY").get()
    # Use api_key securely here

with Flow("secure-flow") as flow:
    use_secret()
```

Scoped Access and Versioning Prefect's secrets are scoped per workspace and environment, facilitating controlled access and separation between development, staging, and production contexts. Versioning within Prefect allows seamless secret rotation by updating the secret value behind the same key without changing the flow definitions.

Integration Synergy Prefect secrets can be used in conjunction with external secret managers by storing tokens or minimal credentials in Prefect and delegating heavier secret retrieval logic to task code. This hybrid approach provides maximum flexibility with layers of security.

General Best Practices in Secrets Management

- **Avoid Hardcoding Secrets**: Do not embed any credentials, tokens, or API keys directly in source code repositories or flow definitions. Rely exclusively on secret managers or environment variables injected securely at runtime.

- **Enforce Least Privilege**: Secrets should grant only the minimal permissions required for tasks to function. When integrating with Vault or AWS Secrets Manager, define narrow policies or IAM roles to limit the blast radius of compromised credentials.

- **Ensure Auditability and Monitoring**: Use secret management solutions' audit logging features to track secret access patterns. This monitoring aids compliance and rapid incident response.

- **Secure Transmission and Storage**: Ensure secure network channels (e.g., TLS) between Prefect agents and secret management endpoints. Utilize encryption-at-rest features inherent in secrets solutions.

- **Automate Rotation and Revocation**: Credential rotation reduces exposure windows. Embed logic in Prefect flows or deployment pipelines to handle secret refresh events gracefully and revoke expired credentials promptly.

Incorporating these robust secrets management techniques into Prefect workflows guarantees sensitive credentials remain protected throughout their lifecycle, preserving system integrity and enabling secure, compliant automation at scale.

5.4. DevOps Automation: CI/CD Integration

Continuous Integration and Continuous Deployment (CI/CD) pipelines form the backbone of modern DevOps practices, enabling frequent and reliable software delivery through automation. Prefect's dataflow orchestration framework integrates seamlessly into these pipelines, providing robust workflow management that elevates automation beyond traditional CI/CD tasks. This section details the practical embedding of Prefect workflows within CI/CD systems such as GitHub Actions and Jenkins, facilitating a DevOps-driven approach to orchestration.

Prefect workflows, defined as Directed Acyclic Graphs (DAGs) of tasks, represent complex data or infrastructure processes that benefit from automated execution triggered by source control events or scheduled pipeline jobs. Integrating Prefect into a CI/CD toolchain enables verification, deployment, and operationalization of workflows in a reproducible and scalable manner.

Embedding Prefect Workflows in GitHub Actions

GitHub Actions is a widely adopted CI/CD platform that automates software workflows directly through YAML configuration files stored in the repository. Prefect workflows can be executed or deployed within these actions to streamline orchestration alongside code build, test, and release stages.

Consider a repository hosting Prefect flow scripts for an ETL process. A typical GitHub Actions workflow (.github/workflows/main.yml) integrates Prefect execution as follows:

```
name: Prefect Workflow CI/CD

on:
  push:
    branches: [main]
  workflow_dispatch:

jobs:
  deploy-and-run:
    runs-on: ubuntu-latest

    steps:
    - uses: actions/checkout@v3

    - name: Set up Python
      uses: actions/setup-python@v4
      with:
        python-version: '3.9'

    - name: Install Dependencies
      run: |
        python -m pip install --upgrade pip
        pip install prefect[all]

    - name: Run Prefect Flow
      run: |
        prefect deployment build etl_flow.py:etl_flow -n "daily-
    etl-deployment"
        prefect deployment apply daily-etl-deployment.yaml
        prefect deployment run "etl_flow/daily-etl-deployment"
```

This CI workflow executes upon pushes to the main branch or manual triggers. The defined jobs perform the following:

- **Checkout Code**: Retrieves the latest source including Prefect flow definitions.

- **Python Environment Setup**: Ensures a consistent runtime.

- **Dependency Installation**: Installs Prefect and any package extras required.

- **Prefect Workflow Lifecycle**: Builds a deployment from the flow script, applies the deployment configuration, and triggers execution.

This automated cycle guarantees that only verified, up-to-date orchestration workflows are deployed and executed in the target environment. The declarative nature of GitHub Actions workflow files also permits easy parameterization and environment management.

Prefect Integration with Jenkins Pipelines

Jenkins, a long-established automation server, allows declarative and scripted pipelines written in Groovy. Prefect workflows can similarly be integrated to trigger flow executions and deployment management as pipeline stages.

Below is a snippet of a Jenkins scripted pipeline utilizing Prefect CLI commands:

```
pipeline {
    agent any

    stages {
        stage('Checkout') {
            steps {
                checkout scm
            }
        }
```

```
stage('Setup Python') {
    steps {
        sh '''
        python3 -m venv venv
        source venv/bin/activate
        pip install --upgrade pip
        pip install prefect[all]
        '''
    }
}

stage('Deploy Prefect Flow') {
    steps {
        sh '''
        source venv/bin/activate
        prefect deployment build flows/etl_flow.py:
etl_flow -n "jenkins-etl-deployment"
        prefect deployment apply jenkins-etl-deployment.
yaml
        '''
    }
}

stage('Run Prefect Flow') {
    steps {
        sh '''
        source venv/bin/activate
        prefect deployment run etl_flow/jenkins-etl-
deployment
        '''
    }
}
}

post {
    always {
        cleanWs()
    }
}
}
```

The pipeline stages correspond to code checkout, environment stabilization, deployment creation, and execution invocation. By managing Prefect workflows as code within Jenkins, cross-team orchestration benefits from Jenkins' robust integration ecosystem, including credential management, notifications, and multibranch pipelines.

127

Considerations for Production-Grade CI/CD Integration

Integrating Prefect into DevOps pipelines involves several considerations to ensure operational stability and observability:

- **Authentication and Security**: Prefect Cloud and Prefect Orion APIs require authentication tokens, securely injected into builds via environment variables or secrets management plugins. Avoid hardcoding tokens in pipeline scripts.

- **Idempotent Deployments**: Repeated deployments should produce consistent states. This can be achieved by version pinning and explicit deployment names to avoid needless re-creation of artifacts.

- **Parameterization and Environment Configs**: Use pipeline inputs or environment variables to pass dynamic parameters to Prefect flows, enabling customization without changing source code.

- **Error Handling and Notifications**: Incorporate failure condition checks on Prefect CLI commands and surface comprehensive logs as pipeline artifacts or via message integrations (e.g., Slack or email).

- **Scaling and Agent Management**: For heavy or parallel workloads, integrate pipeline steps to provision or scale Prefect agents dynamically, matching compute to workflow demands.

Operationalizing Prefect Flows in CI/CD Context

The strength of Prefect in CI/CD pipelines lies in its orchestration abstraction, which complements standard software lifecycle controls by managing task dependencies, retries, caching, and state transitions. As flows are versioned artifacts, their automated testing and deployment embedded in CI/CD pipelines enforce quality gates, making data workflows first-class citizens in DevOps processes.

Centralizing deployments in the pipeline also facilitates compliance, as all flow changes and executions are traceable through repository commits and pipeline run histories. Additionally, the Prefect UI or CLI can be linked as a downstream step or manual promotion gate, enabling on-demand monitoring or approval workflows.

The integration of Prefect with CI/CD platforms such as GitHub Actions and Jenkins transforms orchestration workflows from isolated scripts into managed, production-ready components of the software delivery lifecycle. By embedding deployment and execution commands into pipeline definitions, teams achieve automated, repeatable, and auditable flow management that aligns with DevOps principles. Prefect's flexibility allows seamless adoption within existing toolchains, elevating data and infrastructure orchestration to the standard of continuous delivery and operational resilience.

5.5. Kubernetes and Container Orchestration

Containerization fundamentally transforms workflow deployment by encapsulating applications and their dependencies into lightweight, portable units. Kubernetes extends this paradigm by offering a robust platform for orchestrating containerized workloads at scale, ensuring resource isolation, automated deployment, and seamless management. For Prefect workloads, which involve declarative workflow definitions and dynamic execution, the integration with Kubernetes enables efficient and scalable orchestration within cloud or on-premise clusters.

Prefect workflows can be containerized by defining each task or flow in a Docker image that bundles necessary dependencies and execution logic. The key is to ensure that these images are de-signed to run autonomously and leverage Kubernetes-native features such as ConfigMaps, Secrets, and persistent volumes for configuration and data management.

Deploying Prefect workloads on Kubernetes typically involves the use of the Prefect Kubernetes Agent. This agent listens for flow runs scheduled through the Prefect orchestration API and launches jobs in the cluster using the specified container images. Each FlowRun corresponds to a Kubernetes Pod which isolates resources and runs workflows to completion. To enable this, a declarative YAML manifest specifies the Pod configuration, encapsulating CPU, memory requests, and other constraints.

Because Kubernetes supports declarative configuration, the scheduling and lifecycle of Prefect flows benefit from clear versioning, auditable manifests, and reproducibility. Leveraging the Kubernetes API, Prefect can dynamically scale up or down the number of running Pods in response to workflow demand, supporting parallelism and robust failure handling.

Helm is the de facto package manager for Kubernetes, stream-lining the deployment and management of complex applications through templated manifests and release management. Prefect provides a Helm chart that abstracts the deployment of the Prefect server components (such as the API, UI, and agents) along with associated resource configurations.

Using Helm, administrators can:

- Customize resource allocations (CPU, memory) per Prefect component using parameter overrides.

- Define security contexts, such as RBAC roles and service ac-counts, facilitating fine-grained access control.

- Integrate with external storage or database services by con-figuring persistent volume claims and connection strings.

- Manage upgrades and rollbacks in a controlled manner by recording release history.

For example, deploying the Prefect Helm chart with custom resource requests can be achieved as follows:

```
helm install prefect-release prefecthq/prefect \
  --set server.resources.requests.cpu=500m \
  --set server.resources.requests.memory=1Gi \
  --set agent.resources.limits.cpu=1 \
  --set agent.resources.limits.memory=2Gi
```

This flexibility ensures that resource consumption aligns with workload requirements and cluster capacity, preventing contention and promoting stability.

Best practices in container orchestration for Prefect workflows include:

- **Immutable Infrastructure and Image Tagging:** To maintain consistency, container images should be tagged with specific version identifiers rather than `latest`. This practice prevents inadvertent drift in environments and guarantees reproducible executions.

- **Resource Quotas and Requests:** Define appropriate resource requests and limits for each Prefect task container. Underprovisioned containers may fail due to lack of CPU or memory, while overprovisioning wastes cluster resources. Kubernetes' Horizontal Pod Autoscaler (HPA) may be employed to dynamically adjust replicas based on workload metrics.

- **Namespace Isolation and RBAC:** Deploy Prefect workloads in dedicated Kubernetes namespaces with tailored RBAC policies. This segmentation enforces security boundaries and prevents interference between unrelated workflows or teams.

- **Persistent Storage Management:** When workflows require durable state or checkpointing, leverage Kubernetes persistent volumes. Use volume claims and storage classes aligned with the cluster infrastructure to ensure data reliability and performance.

- **Logging and Monitoring Integration:** Configure container logs to be forwarded to centralized platforms such as Elasticsearch, Fluentd, or Prometheus. Monitoring Prefect flow metrics and Kubernetes pod performance allows proactive issue detection and capacity planning.

- **Secrets Management:** Use Kubernetes Secrets for sensitive configuration data (API keys, credentials). Avoid baking secrets directly into images. Prefect's configuration can be dynamically loaded via environment variables or mounted volumes at runtime.

- **Graceful Shutdown and Backoff Policies:** Prefect agents should be configured with appropriate termination grace periods to allow running flows to complete or checkpoint safely. Employ Kubernetes backoff and retry policies to handle transient failures in workflow executions.

- **Network Policies and Service Meshes:** Implement network policies to restrict traffic between Prefect components and external services, minimizing attack surface. Integrate with service meshes such as Istio for enhanced observability and control of inter-service communication.

By adhering to these principles, organizations can harness Kubernetes' full capabilities to run Prefect workflows reliably and at scale, addressing operational concerns such as scalability, fault tolerance, and security while minimizing overhead.

The synergy between Prefect and Kubernetes offers a powerful platform for workflow orchestration, combining the declarative and dynamic workflow management features of Prefect with Kubernetes' mature container orchestration tools. Using Helm for deployment expedites repeatable provisioning and upgrade cycles, while careful resource management and security practices ensure dependable, maintainable environments. Containerizing workflows not only promotes portability and consistency but also enables automated scaling, isolation, and optimized resource utilization intrinsic to Kubernetes, making it the preferred choice for building production-grade dataflow pipelines and complex orchestrations.

5.6. Integrating with ML/AI Toolchains

Orchestrating modern machine learning (ML) and artificial intelligence (AI) pipelines demands seamless coordination of diverse components ranging from data ingestion and preprocessing to model training, deployment, and monitoring. Prefect provides a robust framework for managing these workflows with fine-grained control and scalability, enabling data scientists and engineers to focus on model performance rather than infrastructure complexities.

Prefect's flexible task library and intuitive flow abstractions allow integration with widely used ML frameworks and toolchains such as TensorFlow, PyTorch, scikit-learn, and MLflow. This integration capability ensures that each stage, from executing training loops to running batch inference and model retraining, can be defined, scheduled, and monitored programmatically. Prefect's extensibility also facilitates incorporating custom logic for feature engineering, hyperparameter tuning, and validation within the pipeline, preserving reproducibility and traceability.

Connecting Data Ingestion and Feature Engineering

The foundation of any ML pipeline lies in reliable data ingestion and feature engineering. Prefect orchestrates the movement of raw data from sources to feature stores or preprocessing units through modular tasks. For example, tasks can leverage cloud storage APIs (AWS S3, GCP Storage), databases, or streaming platforms like Kafka. Prefect efficiently manages retries and dependency chains in these processes to ensure data consistency and availability.

Once ingested, preprocessing tasks can execute arbitrary transformation code—scaling, normalization, or complex feature extraction—leveraging Prefect's seamless integration with Python libraries such as pandas, NumPy, or Spark. By modeling these steps as Prefect tasks, one can ensure robust execution with fine control over parallelization and resource allocation.

Managing Training Loops and Model Versioning

Central to scaling ML workflows is the effective management of training processes. Prefect enables encapsulating training loops within tasks, whether these run on a local GPU server, distributed cluster, or cloud ML platform. Task parameters can include dataset references, hyperparameters, and checkpoint paths, facilitating experiment tracking and reproducibility.

Here is a conceptual snippet demonstrating a Prefect task wrapping a PyTorch training loop:

```
from prefect import task

@task
def train_model(train_data, val_data, epochs, model_params):
    import torch
    model = MyModel(**model_params)
    optimizer = torch.optim.Adam(model.parameters())
    criterion = torch.nn.CrossEntropyLoss()

    for epoch in range(epochs):
        model.train()
        for inputs, targets in train_data:
            optimizer.zero_grad()
            outputs = model(inputs)
            loss = criterion(outputs, targets)
            loss.backward()
            optimizer.step()
        # Save checkpoint
        torch.save(model.state_dict(), 'model_checkpoint.pth')
```

134

```
# Optionally evaluate on validation data
return 'model_checkpoint.pth'
```

By using Prefect's flow orchestration, such tasks can be linked with data loading and post-training evaluation, controlled via scheduling or triggered by events. Integration with experiment tracking tools like MLflow is straightforward, enabling automatic logging of model parameters, metrics, and artifacts within these tasks.

Pipeline Coordination and Distributed Execution

Complex ML pipelines often run multiple parallel and sequential processes, such as hyperparameter optimization, data augmentation, and nightly retraining. Prefect's dynamic task mapping and conditional branching facilitate scalable pipeline layouts. For distributed execution across heterogeneous environments—Kubernetes clusters, dedicated GPU nodes, or serverless functions—Prefect's infrastructure abstractions ensure that compute resources are appropriately allocated and workflows remain fault-tolerant.

The following listing illustrates setting up a simple flow that chains data preprocessing, model training, and evaluation subflows:

```
from prefect import flow

@flow
def ml_workflow(raw_data_path):
    processed_data = preprocess_data(raw_data_path)
    model_path = train_model(processed_data['train'],
     processed_data['val'], epochs=10, model_params={})
    evaluation_metrics = evaluate_model(model_path,
     processed_data['test'])
    return evaluation_metrics
```

Such orchestration guarantees that any failure in intermediate steps triggers appropriate retries or alerts, preserving pipeline robustness.

Scaling Inference with Workflow Management

135

Beyond training, managing inference at scale is critical. Prefect supports batch and real-time inference scenarios by orchestrating feature retrieval, model loading, and prediction execution. Prefect's event-driven scheduling enables inference pipelines to respond to new data arrivals or user queries promptly.

For instance, serving periodic batch predictions on updated datasets can be scheduled and monitored as flows, ensuring that feature freshness and model versions are consistent. Prefect's integration with cloud services (e.g., AWS Lambda, Azure Functions) allows deploying lightweight Lambda tasks encapsulating inference logic triggered on-demand or by message queues.

Continuous Monitoring and Model Governance

An increasingly important aspect of ML pipelines lies in continuous monitoring for data drift, model decay, and compliance. Prefect facilitates integrating monitoring tasks that periodically validate model performance on production data, compute key performance indicators, and trigger alerts for anomalous behaviors.

Custom monitoring flows can ingest metrics from monitoring frameworks or custom instrumentation and automatically initiate retraining or rollback processes when deviations exceed defined thresholds. This end-to-end governance driven by Prefect's orchestration streamlines MLOps workflows, ensuring reliability and compliance without excessive manual intervention.

Summary of Integration Benefits

Incorporating Prefect into ML/AI toolchains delivers several tangible benefits:

- **Modularity**: Encapsulate disparate pipeline components into reusable tasks.

- **Scalability**: Leverage Prefect's distributed execution for large-scale, resource-intensive workloads.

- **Reproducibility**: Maintain state and results via immutable flow runs and parameterization.

- **Observability**: Monitor pipelines real-time with detailed logs, metrics, and alerts.

- **Flexibility**: Interoperate with cloud-native and on-premises tools seamlessly.

Effectively integrating Prefect enhances team productivity and reliability across the ML lifecycle, enabling data and ML engineering teams to build pipelines that scale from prototype experiments to production-grade deployments with confidence.

Chapter 6

Advanced Features and Customization

Prefect's true value shines when workflows are tailored to meet demanding requirements and evolving workloads. This chapter invites you to explore the outer limits of extensibility—discovering how to build custom tasks, enable dynamic behaviors, and harness the platform's plugin and visualization features to design workflows as unique as your business itself.

6.1. Developing Custom Tasks and Collections

Prefect's core philosophy revolves around modular and composable workflow orchestration, enabling efficient, resilient, and scalable execution. While the built-in tasks cover a wide range of common operations, harnessing the full potential of Prefect frequently necessitates the development of custom tasks and collections tailored to specific domain needs or organizational standards. This approach promotes encapsulation of logic, encourages code reuse, and fosters maintainable pipelines.

Defining Custom Task Classes

At its essence, a Prefect task is a Python class that inherits from the base Task class provided by the prefect library. Custom tasks encapsulate the execution logic within the run method, which Prefect invokes at runtime. To implement a new task, one subclasses Task and provides a specialized run implementation.

```
from prefect import Task

class MultiplyTask(Task):
    def __init__(self, factor: int, **kwargs):
        super().__init__(**kwargs)
        self.factor = factor

    def run(self, x: int) -> int:
        return x * self.factor
```

In this example, MultiplyTask accepts a parameter factor at initialization and multiplies its input x by this factor during execution. The use of constructor arguments facilitates configuration reuse without hardcoding logic.

Parameterization and Context Awareness

Custom tasks can leverage Prefect's context, which includes configuration, runtime metadata, and upstream state information. Accessing context within the run method provides dynamic behavior based on execution conditions or environment variables. This is achievable by importing prefect.context:

```
from prefect import Task, context

class DynamicGreetingTask(Task):
    def run(self) -> str:
        user = context.get("parameters", {}).get("user", "Guest")
        greeting_template = context.get("greeting_template", "
    Hello, {user}!")
        return greeting_template.format(user=user)
```

Utilizing context enables highly flexible task behavior, tailored to runtime inputs or environment-specific configurations, thus enhancing reusable component design.

Error Handling and Retries

Custom tasks can incorporate robust error handling and retry policies by overriding Prefect's native mechanisms or decorating the run function programmatically. Prefect supports automatic retries via the `max_retries` and `retry_delay` parameters during initialization. Tasks may also explicitly handle exceptions:

```python
from prefect import Task
from prefect.engine.signals import FAIL
from datetime import timedelta

class SafeDivideTask(Task):
    def __init__(self, max_retries=3, retry_delay=timedelta(
    seconds=10), **kwargs):
        super().__init__(max_retries=max_retries, retry_delay=
    retry_delay, **kwargs)

    def run(self, numerator: float, denominator: float) -> float:
        try:
            return numerator / denominator
        except ZeroDivisionError:
            self.logger.error("Denominator cannot be zero.")
            raise FAIL("Division by zero encountered")
```

By configuring retries and signaling failure explicitly, tasks achieve graceful error propagation and enhanced resilience within larger flows.

Creating Reusable Collections of Tasks

Beyond crafting individual tasks, it is advantageous to organize logically grouped operations into collections-modules or packages containing complementary tasks, utilities, and abstractions. Collections function as domain-specific libraries, promoting consistency and simplifying maintenance across projects.

A canonical approach is to create a Python package with tasks organized into files by functionality. For instance, one might define a `data_processing` collection:

```python
# data_processing/cleaning.py

from prefect import Task
```

```
class RemoveNullsTask(Task):
    def run(self, data_frame):
        return data_frame.dropna()

class NormalizeTextTask(Task):
    def run(self, text: str) -> str:
        return text.lower().strip()
```

Such collections enable consumers to import tasks explicitly:

```
from data_processing.cleaning import RemoveNullsTask,
    NormalizeTextTask
```

Collections can be extended to encapsulate helper functions, constants, and type definitions, facilitating clean and scalable codebases.

Integration with Prefect Registries and Catalogs

Prefect offers integration points to expose custom task collections within catalog systems or registries, allowing users to discover and share tasks across teams effectively. Packaging task collections for distribution follows standard Python packaging protocols, with the added benefit that tasks become first-class citizens within Prefect's user interface when registered via deployment workflows.

This integration supports automated versioning, semantic compatibility checks, and enhanced observability, encouraging collaborative development practices.

Best Practices for Custom Task Development

Several key recommendations optimize custom task and collection development:

- **Statelessness:** Tasks should maintain statelessness where feasible to maximize concurrent execution and predictability.

- **Input and Output Typing:** Employ type hints to clarify interfaces, which aids validation and discoverability.

- **Declarative Parameters:** Use Prefect's `Parameter` objects and context to decouple runtime configuration from implementation.

- **Logging and Monitoring:** Utilize Prefect's built-in logger within tasks for real-time diagnostics and audit trails.

- **Testing:** Thoroughly unit test custom tasks independently of flows, using mocks for Prefect-specific components if necessary.

- **Documentation:** Maintain clear docstrings and module-level documentation to facilitate adoption and maintenance.

Example: Composite Collection for Data Ingestion

Consider an example collection `data_ingestion` encapsulating tasks for file retrieval, parsing, and validation:

```
# data_ingestion/retrieval.py
from prefect import Task
import requests

class FetchFileTask(Task):
    def run(self, url: str) -> bytes:
        response = requests.get(url)
        response.raise_for_status()
        return response.content

# data_ingestion/parsing.py
from prefect import Task
import pandas as pd
import io

class ParseCSVTask(Task):
    def run(self, file_bytes: bytes) -> pd.DataFrame:
        return pd.read_csv(io.BytesIO(file_bytes))

# data_ingestion/validation.py
from prefect import Task

class ValidateSchemaTask(Task):
    def run(self, df, schema: dict) -> bool:
        for column, dtype in schema.items():
            if column not in df.columns or df[column].dtype !=
        dtype:
```

```
                    raise ValueError(f"Column {column} missing or
        invalid type")
           return True
```

This modular design allows workflows to selectively compose the ingestion pipeline, facilitating reuse and incremental extension.

Developing custom tasks and reusable collections is a powerful extension mechanism that unlocks Prefect's adaptable runtime capabilities. By defining encapsulated, parameterized task classes, leveraging Prefect's contextual features, and organizing logically coherent collections, users build maintainable and shareable components that fit diverse operational contexts. Adhering to best practices in task design ensures reliability, testability, and scalability in complex orchestrations.

6.2. Dynamic and Parameterized Workflows

Dynamic and parameterized workflows represent a paradigm shift from static execution models to adaptable, data-driven orchestration engines capable of responding fluidly to runtime conditions. Unlike rigid workflows predefined with fixed task sequences and parameters, these workflows embrace variability and uncertainty inherent in complex, event-driven environments. They allow the task graph structure, execution parameters, and control flows to evolve dynamically in response to incoming data, external signals, or system states, thus enabling more efficient and resilient process automation.

At the core of dynamic workflows lies the concept of *runtime topology adaptation*. This mechanism enables the workflow to add, omit, or reorder tasks as execution unfolds. Consider an example where task execution depends on the classification of incoming data batches. The initial workflow may trigger a classification task whose output determines subsequent processing branches. The decision points, encoded as conditional nodes or parameterizable control predicates, guide the workflow engine in reshaping the downstream task graph dynamically.

Formally, let $G(V, E)$ be a directed acyclic graph (DAG) representing the static workflow structure with vertices V as tasks and edges E as dependencies. A dynamic topology introduces a family of potential graphs $\{G_i\}$, parameterized by a context vector θ composed of external inputs, internal states, or data-derived features. The evolving execution graph $G(\theta)$ at runtime is selected or constructed through:

$$G(\theta) = \arg\max_{G_i} \pi(G_i \mid \theta)$$

where $\pi(\cdot)$ encodes policy or heuristic rules dictating graph selection based on θ. This formalism highlights that dynamic workflows can be viewed as conditional branching over a meta-space of possible graphs rather than executing a singular fixed graph.

Parameterization extends beyond structure, encompassing task-specific inputs and control flags modulating task behavior. Parameters themselves may be derived from prior task outputs, external event streams, or runtime environment variables, thus closing the loop on data-driven feedback. A practical pattern employs template-based parameter resolution, where placeholders in the workflow specification are resolved by a *parameter provider* module dynamically:

```
def parameter_provider(context):
    # Extracts parameters from context and external signals
    param_alpha = context.get('alpha_threshold', 0.7)
    signal_weight = get_external_signal('weight_factor')
    return {'alpha': param_alpha, 'weight': signal_weight}

def execute_task(parameters):
    alpha = parameters['alpha']
    weight = parameters['weight']
    # Task logic using dynamic parameters
    result = complex_computation(alpha, weight)
    return result
```

Dynamic orchestration in event-driven environments further leverages *event triggers* to initiate or adapt workflows. Event detectors monitor streams or signals, raising triggers that alter the workflow graph or parameter set immediately or at predefined checkpoints. This reactive model fosters responsiveness to real-time conditions such as sensor inputs, user interactions, or service notifications.

Execution engines supporting dynamic workflows typically implement *declarative control schemes* with embedded imperative hooks to incorporate custom logic. For example, a workflow description language or framework may provide constructs like choice, switch, or onEvent blocks allowing compositional event handling and conditional task invocation based on runtime state.

A minimal representative snippet in an orchestration DSL might be:

```
workflow DynamicProcessing {
    task classifyData;
    choice {
        when classifyData.output == 'typeA' -> execute taskA with
        params(paramsA);
        when classifyData.output == 'typeB' -> execute taskB with
        params(paramsB);
        otherwise execute defaultTask;
    }
    onEvent signalReceived -> modifyParameters(newParams);
}
```

This structure ensures that the active workflow paths and parameters respond seamlessly to analytical outcomes and asynchronous events.

To ensure correctness and maintainability amid such dynamism, several engineering practices are recommended. First, maintain explicit versioning of workflow templates and parameter schemas to manage evolving variations. Second, employ validation layers that check parameter coherence and graph consistency before task dispatch. Third, implement monitoring and instrumentation for task outcomes and workflow state transitions, enabling real-time insight and traceability in complex scenarios.

Furthermore, dynamic workflows often benefit from *feedback loops* where results from downstream tasks inform upstream decisions or trigger workflow reconfiguration. This introduces challenges related to state management and potential cyclic dependencies. To address these, frameworks use *stateful task contexts* and *idempotent* task designs that withstand re-execution if triggered by intermediate state changes. Techniques such as checkpointing and compensation mechanisms aid in rolling back partial execution upon unexpected conditions.

In distributed environments, dynamic workflows must reconcile adaptation latency and consistency guarantees. Event-driven triggers may arrive asynchronously and at varying frequencies, necessitating coordination protocols to serialize graph reconfigurations and parameter updates. Workflow orchestrators might employ optimistic concurrency control or transactional state stores to maintain atomicity in updates. Additionally, prioritizing task execution based on dynamic priority weights extracted from parameters or external signals improves resource utilization and responsiveness.

Practical recipes for truly dynamic workflows include:

- **Context-Aware Task Dispatching**: Leverage context propagation to carry parameter values and state metadata through the workflow pipeline. Tasks dynamically select algorithms or adjust computational loads based on this evolving context.

- **Event-Condition-Action (ECA) Patterns**: Embed ECA rules within workflow management to automatically react to external triggers without manual intervention, enabling continuous adaptation.

- **Parameter Inheritance and Overriding**: Use hierarchical parameter scopes where defaults propagate downstream but can be overridden at finer granularities; this supports flexible tuning with minimal redundancy.

- **Graph Mutation Operations**: Provide APIs allowing safe insertion, removal, or substitution of workflow nodes at runtime while preserving dependency invariants.

- **Dynamic Scaling Based on Parameters**: Adjust parallelism degrees, resource allocations, or retry strategies dynamically, informed by runtime metrics included in parameters.

Dynamic and parameterized workflows empower orchestration systems to transcend predetermined designs, embracing runtime intelligence and agility. By interweaving data-driven control flows with responsive parameterization and event-based triggers, these workflows excel in managing complexity and uncertainty characteristic of modern computational landscapes. Integral to their success is a robust framework foundation supporting flexible graph structures, dependable state management, and efficient event handling capabilities.

6.3. Schedules, Time Zones, and Temporal Logic

Advanced scheduling in distributed systems and workflow orchestration requires nuanced handling of temporal constraints to ensure reliable execution of time-sensitive processes. Mastery of recurring flows, interval triggers, time zone awareness, and temporal logic is essential for robust temporal orchestration.

Recurring Flows and Interval Triggers

A recurring flow describes a sequence of operations or tasks that must execute repeatedly according to a specified temporal pattern.

148

Such flows are often defined using cron-like expressions or interval triggers. Interval triggers initiate execution after fixed intervals (e.g., every 15 minutes), while cron expressions enable complex schedules incorporating minute, hour, day-of-month, month, and day-of-week fields.

The choice between interval and cron scheduling depends on the required periodicity and alignment with natural time divisions. For example, a task that must run at the top of every hour requires cron scheduling with a minute field set to zero, while a task triggered every 15 minutes irrespective of clock alignment suits interval triggers.

To implement recurring flows, systems must maintain state about prior executions, next scheduled run time, and adhere to policies governing missed triggers. Strategies for missed triggers include catch-up execution versus skipping missed intervals, both of which have implications for resource usage and data consistency.

Complications in Time Zone Handling

Time zone management is a critical dimension in scheduling, particularly for global applications. Naive scheduling based solely on Coordinated Universal Time (UTC) can lead to execution times that are impractical or misleading to users localized across different geographies.

Temporal workflows need to:

- Support scheduling expressions defined in local time zones.

- Adjust for Daylight Saving Time (DST) transitions.

- Guarantee consistent semantics when clocks shift forward or backward.

A common approach is to store schedules internally in UTC while associating them with a configurable time zone context. During trigger evaluation, conversions between UTC and local time zones use library functions that account for DST rules. For example, a schedule defined as "9:00 AM US Eastern Time" will dynamically map to UTC based on whether DST is active.

DST presents particularly challenging scenarios when clocks jump forward (spring forward) or backward (fall back). Tasks scheduled to run during the missing hour in spring must either be skipped or deferred, whereas those scheduled during the repeated hour in fall may need unique identifiers to avoid double execution.

Temporal Logic for Workflow Orchestration

Beyond simple time-based triggers, temporal logic provides a formal framework for expressing time-dependent constraints and dependencies within workflows. Temporal logic operators such as *Eventually* ($\Diamond$), *Always* ($\Box$), and *Until* (U) can specify properties like "Task B must run eventually after Task A completes" or "Task C must always complete before midnight."

Applying temporal logic to scheduling facilitates:

- Definition of conditional triggers based on the state of prior events.

- Enforcing time-bound constraints and deadlines.

- Reasoning about concurrency and conflicts.

For example, consider a workflow that requires a data consolidation task to trigger only if all sensor data collection tasks have completed within the last hour. Using temporal logic, this condition involves an *Until* operator ensuring that until all data is collected, the consolidation does not start.

Implementing temporal logic in practical orchestrators typically involves augmenting the scheduler with evaluation engines capable of monitoring event streams and evaluating temporal predicates against them. This enables rich, context-aware scheduling decisions responsive to real-time workflow states.

Addressing Real-World Scheduling Challenges

Real-world scheduling must handle complexities such as task drift, clock skew, and varying process latencies. Drift refers to cumulative deviations in scheduled execution times caused by system delays or execution overruns. Clock skew-differences in time readings across distributed system nodes-complicates synchronization of schedules.

To mitigate drift, robust schedulers employ recalibration techniques that realign subsequent executions to their intended schedule times rather than relying on the completion time of previous runs. This maintains alignment with real-world time boundaries.

For clock skew, consensus protocols or external synchronization services like NTP (Network Time Protocol) are typically used to maintain consistent time references across nodes. Scheduling frameworks can then rely on synchronized clocks for trigger evaluation.

Additionally, workflows may require "rate limiting" or "backoff" strategies to control scheduling frequency dynamically based on system load or failure conditions. This introduces adaptive temporal behavior, integrating temporal logic with system metrics to optimize throughput and stability.

```
from croniter import croniter
from datetime import datetime
import pytz

# Define schedule in US Eastern Time
eastern = pytz.timezone('US/Eastern')
cron_expression = '0 9 * * *'  # At 09:00 AM every day

# Current time in UTC
now_utc = datetime.utcnow().replace(tzinfo=pytz.utc)

# Convert to Eastern time
now_eastern = now_utc.astimezone(eastern)
```

```
# Create cron iterator based on local time
cron = croniter(cron_expression, now_eastern)

# Next scheduled time in Eastern
next_run_local = cron.get_next(datetime)

# Convert back to UTC for execution
next_run_utc = eastern.localize(next_run_local.replace(tzinfo=
    None)).astimezone(pytz.utc)

print(f"Next run local time: {next_run_local}")
print(f"Next run UTC time: {next_run_utc}")
```

```
Next run local time: 2024-06-01 09:00:00
Next run UTC time: 2024-06-01 13:00:00+00:00
```

Combining these techniques allows the design of temporal orchestration systems capable of managing complex time-dependent workflows with high precision and reliability. Proper handling of schedules, time zones, and temporal logic forms the backbone of practical, production-grade temporal management in modern distributed and cloud-native environments.

6.4. Hooks, Callbacks, and Event Subscriptions

Prefect's orchestration framework provides powerful mechanisms to extend workflows beyond their core execution logic by reacting dynamically to lifecycle events. These mechanisms include hooks, callbacks, and event subscriptions, which collectively enable integration with external systems, automated responses to execution states, and customized logging or alerting strategies. The ability to seamlessly intertwine workflows with ancillary processes is crucial for robust automation pipelines and enterprise-grade reliability.

Hooks in Prefect represent user-defined logic attached to specific points in a task or flow lifecycle. They act as interception points, running custom code when certain events occur, for example, when a task starts, succeeds, fails, or retries. Hooks are implemented as method overrides or as decorators and offer fine-grained control to inject behavior directly into the execution sequence. Prefect tasks expose a set of predefined lifecycle methods, such as `on_start`, `on_success`, and `on_failure`, upon which hooks can be registered.

Callbacks, a concept closely related to hooks, are functions or callables triggered by lifecycle events but are often registered externally to the core task code, providing modular extension without modifying task definitions. Prefect supports attaching callbacks at the flow or task level, enabling observers to subscribe to execution states and execute custom logic accordingly.

For example, monitoring notifications can be implemented by registering a callback that sends an alert to a messaging platform upon a task's failure. Similarly, data validation steps can be triggered post-task success via callbacks.

Prefect flows emit an extensive range of event signals associated with workflow and task state transitions. These events represent state changes such as `Scheduled`, `Running`, `Completed`, `Failed`, or `Skipped`. Prefect's event bus architecture allows subscribers to listen to these events and act in real time as workflows evolve.

Subscribing to lifecycle events operates on a publish-subscribe model, where hooks and callbacks act as subscribers, and the flow's execution engine publishes events. This model decouples event handling logic from core workflow definitions, enhancing maintainability and scalability.

In practice, subscription to flow lifecycle events can be implemented via Prefect's state handlers. A state handler is a callable accepting the current and new state of a task or flow; it returns the state to continue execution or modify the flow based on the event. By assigning state handlers, workflows gain the ability to automatically trigger external integrations, rollbacks, or compensating actions based on event-driven conditions.

Consider a scenario where a data ingestion pipeline requires automated alerting to an operations team when a key extraction task fails. By attaching a failure hook to the extraction task, an alert can be dispatched as soon as the failure event is emitted, reducing mean time to detection.

The following example shows a custom failure hook integrated into a Prefect task implementation:

```
from prefect import task
import requests

def notify_failure(task, state):
    if state.is_failed():
        payload = {
            "text": f"Task {task.name} failed with error: {state.
        message}"
        }
        requests.post("https://hooks.slack.com/services/XXX/YYY/
        ZZZ", json=payload)

@task(state_handlers=[notify_failure])
def extract_data():
    # Extraction logic that might fail
    pass
```

In this snippet, the function notify_failure acts as a state handler monitoring the task's lifecycle. If the task transitions into a failure state, a JSON payload is posted to a Slack webhook URL to alert the team. The elegant use of state handlers here avoids hardcoding notification logic into task internals, maintaining separation of concerns.

Beyond notifications, hooks and callbacks can initiate more complex external processes such as triggering downstream workflows, updating dashboards, or reconciling data stores. By subscribing to key lifecycle events, workflows can programmatically drive distributed automation architectures.

Prefect flows can register global state handlers that monitor all tasks, enabling broad event observation and reaction. For example, a global handler can trigger a REST API call to an orchestration dashboard each time a flow enters a terminal state-this ensures up-to-date status visualization without manual interference.

```
from prefect import Flow

def flow_status_update(flow, old_state, new_state):
    if new_state.is_final():
        requests.post(
            "https://api.dashboard.example.com/update",
            json={"flow_id": flow.id, "status": str(new_state)}
        )
    return new_state

with Flow("data_pipeline", state_handlers=[flow_status_update])
    as flow:
    # task definitions
    pass
```

Here, the `flow_status_update` handler intercepts flow state transitions, only triggering external API calls when final states are reached, such as `Completed` or `Failed`. This pattern enables automated auditing, compliance triggers, and integration with third-party monitoring services.

When leveraging hooks, callbacks, and event subscriptions, it is essential to manage potential side effects. Handlers should be idempotent, performant, and resilient to failures; otherwise, they risk cascading issues within critical workflows. Employing asynchronous request patterns and robust error handling within callbacks protects primary workflow execution from latency or disruption caused by external systems.

Security considerations also apply when integrating with external endpoints. Prefect workflows should use encrypted channels, authentication tokens, and adhere to least-privilege principles to prevent unauthorized access due to event-driven interactions.

Lastly, the design of hook and callback logic must align with the overall workflow architecture. Overuse of callbacks, or event-heavy workflows without clear separation, can increase complexity and hinder maintainability. Clear documentation and modular coding conventions mitigate these risks.

- **Hooks** embed custom logic within task lifecycle stages, enabling fine-grained control over execution.

- **Callbacks** provide externally registered functions reacting to flow or task events, facilitating modular extension.

- **Event subscriptions** rely on state handlers and Prefect's event bus to respond appropriately to lifecycle state transitions.

Collectively, these constructs empower engineers to implement reactive workflows that integrate smoothly with enterprise monitoring, automation, and alerting ecosystems. The ability to programmatically respond to workflow transitions ensures operational agility, faster incident response, and higher reliability in automated data and application pipelines.

6.5. Prefect API Extensions and Plugin Architecture

Prefect's extensibility is a fundamental feature that enables tailored orchestration solutions to be built upon its robust core. Extending Prefect with custom plugins and API integrations amplifies its adaptability by enabling users to infuse domain-specific logic and third-party services into workflows. This section explores the architecture and practical mechanisms for extending Prefect through its API and plugin system, emphasizing how to harness these tools to introduce new functionalities, enhance automation, and facilitate rapid innovation.

At the heart of Prefect's extensibility lies its REST API, which orchestrates communication between the Prefect server components and client interfaces. This API exposes endpoints for managing flows, deployments, flow runs, task runs, agents, and more, enabling users to programmatically control and query the state of workflow executions. The API serves not only as a control plane but also as an integration point for external systems. By developing custom clients or augmenting the existing ones, developers can embed Prefect's capabilities into broader infrastructure ecosystems.

Interacting with Prefect's API programmatically typically involves leveraging the Prefect Python client library, which abstracts API calls into convenient method calls. However, for more specialized use cases or language interoperability requirements, direct HTTP requests can be constructed using RESTful principles. For instance, creating a flow run via the API involves a POST request to the /flow_runs endpoint with a properly structured JSON payload specifying the flow deployment and parameters.

```python
import requests

api_url = "https://api.prefect.io/flow_runs"
api_token = "YOUR_API_TOKEN"

headers = {
    "Authorization": f"Bearer {api_token}",
    "Content-Type": "application/json"
}

payload = {
    "deployment_id": "deployment-uuid",
    "parameters": {
        "param1": "value1"
    }
}

response = requests.post(api_url, json=payload, headers=headers)
print(response.json())
```

```
{
    "id": "flow-run-uuid",
    "flow_id": "flow-uuid",
    "deployment_id": "deployment-uuid",
    "state": {"type": "State", "name": "Scheduled"},
    ...
}
```

Building on this API foundation, Prefect accommodates plugin development through a modular architecture designed to introduce new task types, extend the scheduler, customize the logging and monitoring system, or integrate alternative storage and notification services. Plugins are Python packages that implement standardized interfaces or inherit from Prefect base classes, enabling seamless integration without altering the core codebase.

A typical Prefect plugin manifests as a subclass of a well-defined hook or plugin base class, such as custom task implementations subclassing `prefect.Task` or a new infrastructure connector deriving from `prefect.infrastructure.BaseInfrastructure`. The plugin registration mechanism is declarative, often utilizing entry points in Python's packaging system (`setup.py` or `pyproject.toml`) to declare the plugin's availability. When Prefect launches, it discovers these entry points to register additional functionalities dynamically.

For example, to develop a plugin introducing a custom task that performs encrypted data transfer, a user would subclass the `Task` class and override its run method:

```python
from prefect import Task

class EncryptedTransferTask(Task):
    def __init__(self, encryption_key: str, **kwargs):
        self.encryption_key = encryption_key
        super().__init__(**kwargs)

    def run(self, source_path: str, destination_path: str):
        # Implement encryption logic here
        encrypted_data = self.encrypt(source_path)
        self.transfer(encrypted_data, destination_path)

    def encrypt(self, path):
        # Encryption code utilizing self.encryption_key
        pass

    def transfer(self, data, dest):
        # Transfer encrypted data to destination
        pass
```

Proper packaging of this task as a plugin allows users to include it seamlessly in their Prefect flows, enabling reusability and encapsulation of complex logic. Additionally, combining this with API extensions enables automation triggered by external systems or event sources, expanding orchestration beyond Prefect-native workflows.

To integrate third-party functionality, the plugin architecture facilitates connections to popular tools and services. For instance, plugins can implement custom notification mechanisms compatible with Slack, Microsoft Teams, or email services, using Prefect's existing event hooks to trigger notifications on lifecycle events such as flow completion or task failure. Similarly, new storage blocks or secret providers may be added by implementing Prefect's block interfaces, enabling secure and efficient management of workflow credentials and data artifacts.

The interaction between Prefect's core, the API, and plugins promotes rapid iteration and innovation. Developers can introduce new features without waiting for upstream contributions, experiment with novel integrations in isolation, and share modular components within organizations. This accelerates time-to-value and enables sophisticated automation scenarios, such as AI-driven workflow adaptations or complex event-driven pipelines combining diverse SaaS APIs.

From an architectural perspective, preferring loosely coupled plugins accessed via standardized APIs reduces maintenance overhead and fosters a robust ecosystem. The modular approach also improves testability, as plugins can be independently validated against mock API environments or staging Prefect instances. Versioning strategies at both the API and plugin levels further ensure compatibility and smooth upgrades.

Prefect's extensibility through its API and plugin architecture empowers users to customize the orchestration platform according to domain-specific requirements, incorporate third-party services, and drive continuous innovation. Mastery of these mechanisms is essential for engineers aiming to harness Prefect's full potential in creating scalable, automated, and adaptive data workflows.

6.6. Visualization, Dashboards, and User Interfaces

Effective orchestration of data workflows requires not only reliable execution of tasks but also the ability to monitor, visualize, and interact with these workflows. Visualization, dashboards, and user interfaces serve as critical components in translating complex operational data into actionable insights. This section explores the design and implementation of insightful workflow visualizations, custom dashboards, and operational portals, emphasizing both Prefect's built-in capabilities and best practices for constructing tailored observability platforms that meet organizational requirements.

Prefect provides a foundational observability experience through its Cloud UI and Prefect Orion server, which collectively offer real-time status tracking, flow run histories, task-level details, and event logs. The built-in interface employs a graph-based visualization of workflows, depicting flow run states, task dependencies, and execution timelines. This visualization leverages the Directed Acyclic Graph (DAG) structure inherent to Prefect flows, enabling users to intuitively comprehend execution paths and identify bottlenecks or failure points.

The core visual elements include:

- **Flow Graphs**: Visual representations of the flow DAG display nodes as task runs and edges as dependencies. Color-coding and icons indicate status such as success, running, failed, or skipped.

- **Run Timelines**: Gantt-chart style timelines illustrate the start and end times for each task, facilitating the detection of long-running or stalled tasks.

- **Logs and Events**: Integration with the logging system allows users to drill down into detailed log entries and emitted events, providing context for troubleshooting.

While Prefect's native UI is comprehensive, it is sometimes necessary to construct custom dashboards or operational portals that
align with specific organizational workflows, business metrics, or
user roles. Customization may involve aggregating data from multiple flows, integrating with external systems, or presenting simplified user views. Approaches to building such user-facing observability platforms can be broadly categorized as follows:

API-Driven Custom Visualization

Prefect's REST API exposes extensive endpoints to retrieve flow,
flow run, and task run metadata, including states, logs, and parameters. Leveraging this API, teams can programmatically gather
workflow telemetry and build bespoke web interfaces or embed live
status components into existing enterprise portals.

A typical architecture involves:

- Polling or subscribing to state change events via the Prefect
  API or webhook mechanisms.

- Persisting aggregated data in a dedicated time-series or document database optimized for query performance.

- Employing visualization frameworks (e.g., D3.js, React, or
  Grafana) to generate dynamic charts, status indicators, and
  interactive graphs.

Particular attention should be given to caching strategies and
event-driven updates to maintain interface responsiveness without overloading the Prefect backend.

Embedding Observability in Operational Portals

Operational personnel often require views tailored by responsibilities, focusing on areas such as SLA adherence, error management,

or throughput metrics. Embedding Prefect observability within broader operational portals can be achieved by combining workflow metadata with business KPIs.

Design considerations include:

- **Role-Based Access**: Ensure that user interfaces respect authentication and authorization constraints, exposing only relevant data according to user roles.

- **Aggregated Metrics**: Summarize workflow execution metrics such as success rates, average durations, and error counts over configurable periods.

- **Alerting and Anomaly Visualization**: Integrate workflow alerts (e.g., task failures, SLA breaches) with visual indicators or notifications to drive proactive incident resolution.

Using frameworks like Dash, Streamlit, or enterprise-grade BI tools allows rapid prototyping and deployment of these operational views.

Workflow-Specific Visualizations

Some organizations benefit from creating domain-specific visualizations that map workflow execution data onto business processes or operational states. For example, in a supply chain context, visualizing the progress of order fulfillment workflows alongside inventory or shipping data enhances decision making.

Techniques include:

- Mapping task states to domain entities or geographical locations via custom markers or heatmaps.

- Correlating Prefect runtime metrics with external system telemetry to provide holistic situational awareness.

- Implementing drill-down capabilities that allow users to navigate from high-level summaries to task-level details seamlessly.

Best Practices in Visual Interface Design for Observability

- **Clarity and Minimalism**: Visualizations should minimize cognitive load by presenting only essential information and using consistent color palettes to differentiate status states.

- **Interactivity**: Allowing users to filter, search, and explore data enhances engagement and expedites problem diagnosis.

- **Real-Time Updates**: Near real-time reflection of workflow states increases situational awareness but must be balanced against resource utilization.

- **Contextual Information**: Supplement visual elements with metadata, such as task parameters, execution environment, or error stack traces, accessible on demand.

- **Consistency Across Platforms**: Uniformity between Prefect native UI representations and custom dashboards fosters a seamless user experience.

Example: Fetching Flow Run Statuses through the Prefect API

The following Python snippet illustrates fetching the latest statuses of flow runs using Prefect's API client. This data can serve as the foundation for custom visualizations or dashboards.

```
import asyncio
from prefect.client import get_client

async def fetch_flow_runs(flow_id, limit=10):
    async with get_client() as client:
        flow_runs = await client.read_flow_runs(
            flow_filter={"flow_id": {"any_": [flow_id]}},
```

```
            limit=limit,
            sort={"field": "START_TIME", "order": "DESCENDING"},
        )
        return flow_runs

# Example usage in an async context
# flow_id = "your-flow-uuid"
# flow_runs = asyncio.run(fetch_flow_runs(flow_id))
# for run in flow_runs:
#     print(f"Run ID: {run.id}, State: {run.state.type}, Started:
        {run.start_time}")
```

```
Run ID: 123e4567-e89b-12d3-a456-426614174000, State: Completed, Started: 2024
-06-12T15:30:45Z
Run ID: 123e4567-e89b-12d3-a456-426614174001, State: Failed, Started: 2024-06
-12T14:10:21Z
...
```

Integrating such programmatically obtained status information into web interfaces or mobile applications enables organizations to construct focused monitoring portals aligned with their operational workflows.

Constructing effective visualization, dashboards, and user interfaces for workflow observability in Prefect involves a combination of leveraging the platform's native tools and extending them with custom-built solutions. These interfaces not only contribute to operational transparency but also empower stakeholders to make informed decisions through timely and contextual insights tailored to diverse organizational roles and needs.

Chapter 7

Security, Compliance, and Governance

In today's data-driven world, workflow orchestration isn't just about moving bytes—it's about doing so with trust and accountability. This chapter delves into the foundations of secure orchestration, covering access control, encryption, auditability, and adherence to global compliance frameworks. Learn how Prefect ensures your workflows are not only powerful but also safe, transparent, and policy-compliant from the ground up.

7.1. Authentication, Authorization, and Role-based Control

Prefect's architecture emphasizes comprehensive security measures through layered access controls, ensuring that workflows and infrastructure remain protected against unauthorized use or malicious interference. The triad of authentication, authorization, and role-based access control (RBAC) forms the cornerstone for safeguarding Prefect deployments. Each mechanism addresses specific security requirements that, when combined, establish a robust governance framework.

Authentication in Prefect

Authentication verifies the identity of users and services attempting to access Prefect's API, UI, and underlying systems. Prefect supports several authentication strategies designed for integration flexibility and security assurance:

- **API Key Authentication**: Prefect agents and clients use API keys to authenticate against the Prefect server. These keys are cryptographically strong tokens generated per user or service, minimizing the exposure of sensitive credentials. API keys are transmitted over secure channels (TLS), and their scope and expiration can be configured for enhanced control.

- **Single Sign-On (SSO) and OAuth**: Enterprises often integrate Prefect with existing identity providers (IdPs) via OAuth 2.0 or SAML-based SSO. This enables centralized user management, multifactor authentication, and compliance with organizational security policies.

- **Local User Authentication**: For simpler deployments, Prefect supports username-password authentication managed internally. Passwords are stored in hashed form, following best practices such as the Argon2 or bcrypt algorithms, ensuring the protection of user credentials.

Effective authentication reduces risk vectors by strictly verifying identity before any resource access, providing the foundation upon which authorization and role enforcement operate.

Granular Authorization Mechanisms

Authorization governs the actions authenticated users and services are allowed to perform within the Prefect ecosystem. Prefect's authorization model applies fine-grained rules to ensure that users gain only the privileges necessary to execute their workflows or administer related infrastructure components.

- **Resource-Level Access**: Prefect defines permissions at various resource levels such as flows, flow runs, blocks, and work queues. Users or service principals can be granted read, write, or administrative privileges on these entities. This granularity enables segregation of duties; for example, a team member may trigger runs but not alter critical flow definitions.

- **Token Scopes**: API tokens include scope restrictions specifying allowed operations. This limits the damage potential if a token is compromised by bounding it to read-only access or specific namespace operations.

- **Time-Based and Contextual Controls**: Advanced authorization configurations support time-limited access as well as contextual conditions such as IP whitelisting. This reduces the attack surface by restricting the temporal and network context under which permissions are valid.

Authorization policies can be expressed declaratively or managed via the Prefect UI/API, ensuring administrators can tailor access rules according to organizational needs and compliance requirements.

Role-Based Access Control (RBAC)

Prefect employs RBAC to simplify management of user permissions in complex environments where multiple users or teams interact with overlapping resources.

- **Role Definitions**: Roles encapsulate a set of permissions aligned with typical job functions-e.g., Reader, Operator,

167

`Admin`. This abstraction reduces the complexity of individually assigning permissions and minimizes human error.

- **Hierarchical Role Structure**: Roles can be composed hierarchically, allowing inheritance of permissions. For instance, an `Admin` role includes all privileges of `Operator` and `Reader` roles, enabling consistent escalation models.

- **Namespace Isolation**: Roles can be scoped within namespaces, creating isolated security domains. This model supports multi-tenant architectures where distinct teams or applications operate independently within the same Prefect deployment.

- **Dynamic Assignment and Auditing**: Users and service principals can be dynamically bound to roles through automated identity management workflows. Prefect maintains detailed audit logs documenting assignment changes and access events, facilitating compliance audits and forensic investigations.

Implementing RBAC ensures that the principle of least privilege is systematically enforced, significantly decreasing insider threat exposure and operational mistakes.

Integration with Workflow Security

Authentication, authorization, and RBAC directly influence how Prefect manages execution of workflows and safeguards underlying infrastructure.

- **Agent Authentication**: Prefect agents require valid credentials to register and communicate with the orchestration server. This prevents unauthorized code execution on computational resource pools.

- **Run-Time Permission Checks**: At the initiation of each flow run, Prefect verifies that the invoking identity has permissions matching the action requested (e.g., submit, cancel, view logs). This real-time enforcement protects against privilege escalation within operational lifecycles.

- **Secret and Block Access**: Sensitive data such as API keys, database credentials, or cloud provider tokens are managed through Prefect blocks with carefully controlled access policies. Only authorized roles and users can retrieve these secrets, which are never exposed in plaintext.

Enforcing Security Policies Across Layers

Security in Prefect extends beyond authentication and authorization at the API/UI level to encompass infrastructure and data handling layers:

- **Transport Security**: All communications between clients, agents, and the Prefect server utilize TLS encryption to protect data in transit.

- **Storage Encryption**: Sensitive data stored within Prefect's backend, such as metadata and secrets, employ encryption at rest with strong key management.

- **Infrastructure Access Controls**: Integration with platform-level identity and access management (IAM) systems allows unified control over nodes, databases, and cloud resources, ensuring that Prefect users cannot circumvent workflow-level controls by accessing lower layers directly.

Prefect's multi-layered approach enforces authentication, authorization, and role-based controls to secure workflows, protect data, and maintain compliance with enterprise security standards. Its configurable and extensible model facilitates deployment in diverse environments, from single-team setups to large-scale, multitenant systems, without compromising operational agility or governance.

7.2. Network Security and Data Encryption

Securing data in Prefect environments necessitates a comprehensive approach that encompasses both data in-transit and data at-rest. Given Prefect's distributed architecture, where orchestration commands, state updates, and data artifacts traverse multiple network boundaries, robust security controls are essential to maintain confidentiality, integrity, and availability.

Transport Layer Security: TLS/SSL Integration

TLS (Transport Layer Security), along with its predecessor SSL (Secure Sockets Layer), forms the cornerstone for securing data in-transit within Prefect environments. Prefect's communication channels-APIs, agents, and cloud services-must leverage TLS to encrypt data packets, preventing eavesdropping and man-in-the-middle attacks.

A typical setup involves enabling TLS on all Prefect server endpoints. For deployments on Kubernetes or cloud platforms, this entails provisioning certificates from trusted Certificate Authorities (CAs) or utilizing internally managed Public Key Infrastructure (PKI). The Prefect server's API gateway or ingress controller should be configured to require and enforce HTTPS connections. An exemplary snippet for enabling TLS in an NGINX ingress controller might look like this:

```
apiVersion: networking.k8s.io/v1
kind: Ingress
metadata:
  name: prefect-ingress
  annotations:
    nginx.ingress.kubernetes.io/ssl-redirect: "true"
spec:
  tls:
  - hosts:
      - prefect.example.com
    secretName: prefect-tls-secret
  rules:
  - host: prefect.example.com
    http:
      paths:
```

```
- path: /
  pathType: Prefix
  backend:
    service:
      name: prefect-server
      port:
        number: 4200
```

This configuration ensures that every connection to the Prefect API server is encrypted. Prefect agents and clients must also support TLS verification, which includes rejecting self-signed or expired certificates unless explicitly trusted.

Additionally, mutual TLS (mTLS) can be employed to authenticate both client and server endpoints, especially in private or high-security environments. This guarantees that only authorized Prefect agents connect to the orchestration backend, mitigating risk from compromised hosts.

Private Network Configurations

Beyond encryption, network isolation provides an additional security layer by restricting communication pathways to only those explicitly permitted. Prefect deployments often benefit from private network architectures such as Virtual Private Clouds (VPCs), private subnets, and firewall rules that limit inbound and outbound traffic.

For example, when deploying Prefect in cloud environments such as AWS, Azure, or GCP, placing the Prefect server instances and agents within private subnets restricts exposure to the public internet. Access to these instances can be granted only through bastion hosts or VPN tunnels. This isolation reduces attack surfaces significantly.

Network policies at the Kubernetes level also enforce granular control. Using Kubernetes Network Policies, administrators can define allowed ingress and egress rules for Pods. A sample NetworkPolicy to restrict Prefect server communication might be:

```
apiVersion: networking.k8s.io/v1
kind: NetworkPolicy
metadata:
  name: allow-prefect-agent
  namespace: prefect
spec:
  podSelector:
    matchLabels:
      app: prefect-server
  ingress:
  - from:
    - podSelector:
        matchLabels:
          app: prefect-agent
    ports:
    - protocol: TCP
      port: 4200
  policyTypes:
  - Ingress
```

This policy enforces that only Pods labeled as `prefect-agent` can communicate with the Prefect server on port 4200, blocking all other ingress traffic.

Data Encryption at Rest

Securing data at-rest involves encrypting stored information such that unauthorized parties cannot access it even if the storage medium is compromised. In Prefect architectures, at-rest data includes workflow logs, execution states, database entries, and potentially data artifacts stored in auxiliary object stores.

Most Prefect components rely on external persistence layers, such as PostgreSQL databases and cloud object storage (e.g., Amazon S3, Google Cloud Storage). These platforms should enable encryption by default or via configuration. Key management becomes crucial; integrating Prefect storage with Key Management Services (KMS), such as AWS KMS or HashiCorp Vault, allows seamless rotation and auditability of encryption keys.

For PostgreSQL, Transparent Data Encryption (TDE) or filesystem-level encryption should be configured on underlying volumes. Example:

```
# AWS EBS volume creation with encryption enabled
aws ec2 create-volume --size 100 --volume-type gp3 --encrypted --
    availability-zone us-east-1a
```

Within object storage, enabling server-side encryption (SSE) is standard practice. Prefect flows often store logs and results here, thus:

```
{
  "Version": "2012-10-17",
  "Statement": [
    {
      "Sid": "EnforceSSE",
      "Effect": "Deny",
      "Principal": "*",
      "Action": "s3:PutObject",
      "Resource": "arn:aws:s3:::prefect-logs/*",
      "Condition": {
        "StringNotEquals": {
          "s3:x-amz-server-side-encryption": "AES256"
        }
      }
    }
  ]
}
```

This bucket policy enforces all uploads to use AES256 encryption, thereby protecting logs at rest.

Cryptographic Controls and Best Practices

Proper implementation of cryptographic controls hinges on adherence to established guidelines for key strength, algorithm selection, and lifecycle management. Prefect environments should enforce:

- Use of strong encryption algorithms such as AES-256 for symmetric encryption and RSA-2048 or ECDSA for asymmetric encryption.

- Enabling perfect forward secrecy (PFS) in TLS configurations by selecting ephemeral Diffie-Hellman key exchange methods (e.g., ECDHE).

- Regular rotation and revocation of encryption keys and certificates to minimize exposure.

- Secure storage of keys and secrets using dedicated vault services, avoiding embedding credentials in code or unencrypted environment variables.

- Enabling HMAC-based integrity verification for message authentication in custom extensions or inter-component communication where applicable.

Prefect's configuration should also restrict protocol versions to TLS 1.2 or above, disallowing obsolete and vulnerable versions such as TLS 1.0 or SSL 3.0. Cipher suites must be selected carefully to exclude weak encryption algorithms and to prioritize AEAD (Authenticated Encryption with Associated Data) modes such as AES-GCM.

Moreover, audit logging for access to cryptographic materials and key usage can support compliance requirements and forensic analysis.

Given Prefect's deployment flexibility-from on-premises to multicloud architectures-security configurations must align with the operational context. Integrating TLS/SSL encryption, deploying within private, segmented networks, and enforcing strong cryptographic controls for data at-rest are crucial pillars in securing workflows.

Automation tools such as Infrastructure as Code (IaC) frameworks can codify these practices consistently. Regular security assessments and penetration testing should verify that the implemented controls withstand evolving threat landscapes.

Together, these strategies frame a resilient and secure Prefect environment that protects sensitive data across its entire lifecycle, ensuring robust operational trustworthiness and compliance with data governance mandates.

7.3. Audit Logging and Traceability

Establishing comprehensive visibility into workflow activity requires a robust framework for audit logging and traceability. These
capabilities form the foundation for operational transparency, ensuring that every action within a system ecosystem is recorded im-
mutably and that the provenance of data and events can be reliably
traced. This approach supports not only internal governance but
also regulatory compliance, forensic analysis, and continuous process improvement.

Audit logs must be designed to provide an indelible and timestamped record of all significant events, including user interactions,
system changes, and automated process executions. The core principle underpinning audit logging is immutability: once an event is
recorded, it must be protected from alteration or deletion. Prac-
tically, this immutability is enforced via cryptographic techniques
such as hashing and chain linking logs, or through append-only
storage mechanisms. For example, storing audit entries in a write-
once, read-many (WORM) medium or employing blockchain-like
structures can ensure an incorruptible history of activities.

- **Event Content and Structure:** Each log entry should encapsulate critical metadata including the identity of the ac-
  tor (user or system component), timestamp, nature of the
  event, affected resources, and if applicable, outcome or status codes. Standardizing log formats such as Common Event
  Format (CEF) or JSON-based structured logs enhances interoperability across monitoring and analysis tools.

- **Provenance Tracking:** Tracking the origin and the lifecycle of data objects and tasks within workflows is integral to
  traceability. Provenance metadata records lineage information, specifying the sequence of derivations, transformations,
  and transfers that data undergoes. This enables verification
  of data integrity, reproducibility of results, and identification

175

of points of failure or anomaly.

- **Correlation and Contextualization:** Effective traceability depends on correlating distributed logs and events across multiple systems and layers. Employing unique identifiers such as transaction IDs or workflow instance IDs that persist throughout the entire process facilitates end-to-end reconstruction of activity flows. Contextual information-such as system configuration versions, environmental states, and user roles at the time of execution-further enriches the trace.

Regular log reviews and continuous monitoring serve as operational controls to detect unauthorized actions, unusual behavior, or system malfunctions. Automated tools can analyze audit logs for patterns indicative of security incidents or operational degradation and generate real-time alerts. Scheduled audits complement these by validating the completeness and integrity of logs, ensuring that audit trails have not been tampered with and comply with organizational policies.

A best practice for managing audit logs involves establishing centralized log aggregation platforms that ingest and normalize data from disparate sources. Coupled with indexing and query capabilities, these platforms enable efficient retrieval and forensic analysis. Indexing critical fields such as timestamps, user IDs, and event types drastically reduces the time required to isolate specific events or timelines during investigations.

```
import hashlib
import json
import time

class AuditLogEntry:
    def __init__(self, actor, event, resource, previous_hash=''):
        self.timestamp = time.time()
        self.actor = actor
        self.event = event
        self.resource = resource
        self.previous_hash = previous_hash
        self.current_hash = self.compute_hash()
```

```
    def compute_hash(self):
        record = json.dumps({
            'timestamp': self.timestamp,
            'actor': self.actor,
            'event': self.event,
            'resource': self.resource,
            'previous_hash': self.previous_hash
        }, sort_keys=True).encode()
        return hashlib.sha256(record).hexdigest()

class AuditLog:
    def __init__(self):
        self.chain = []

    def add_entry(self, actor, event, resource):
        previous_hash = self.chain[-1].current_hash if self.chain
    else ''
        entry = AuditLogEntry(actor, event, resource,
    previous_hash)
        self.chain.append(entry)
        # Persist entry to storage here

    def verify_integrity(self):
        for i in range(1, len(self.chain)):
            if self.chain[i].previous_hash != self.chain[i-1].
    current_hash:
                return False
        return True
```

```
Example output for verifying integrity:
True
```

Provenance tracking also benefits from the use of metadata standards such as the W3C PROV model, which defines entities, activities, and agents alongside their interrelations. By documenting these relationships explicitly, systems can automatize impact analysis, compliance reporting, and rollback procedures where necessary.

In regulated environments, mandates frequently require the maintenance of audit trails that are complete, accurate, and accessible over defined retention periods. This necessitates appropriate policies for log rotation, secure archival, and controlled access mechanisms to ensure that sensitive audit data is protected against unauthorized disclosure or loss while remaining available for permissible examination.

An integrated auditing and traceability infrastructure must align organizational workflow definitions with technical implementation. Instrumenting workflows at points of decision, data transformation, and execution completes the visibility cycle, thus creating a comprehensive record that reflects both the logical and temporal sequences of operations. Together, the mechanisms of immutable audit logging, provenance tracking, and systematic log review enable robust oversight, instill trust in automated processes, and satisfy increasingly stringent accountability demands across industries.

7.4. Compliance Frameworks and Regulatory Considerations

Modern data orchestration platforms such as Prefect operate within a complex regulatory environment where adherence to compliance frameworks is paramount. Organizations must align their Prefect deployments with legal and industry standards including the General Data Protection Regulation (GDPR), Health Insurance Portability and Accountability Act (HIPAA), and System and Organization Controls (SOC 2). This alignment ensures data privacy, security, and operational reliability. A granular understanding of these frameworks, combined with strategic implementation of Prefect's features, enables systematic compliance while maintaining workflow efficiency and agility.

Mapping Prefect Deployments to GDPR requires addressing stringent controls on personal data processing for entities handling data related to European Union (EU) citizens. Key GDPR principles such as data minimization, purpose limitation, transparency, and the right to erasure directly influence the design and execution of data workflows.

Prefect's flow-based architecture supports these principles by enabling explicit definition and control of data lifecycle within workflows. Data minimization can be achieved by leveraging Prefect's parameterization capabilities to restrict data inputs only to what is necessary for processing. Prefect's provenance logging-capturing metadata of flow runs, task states, parameters, and artifacts-provides excellent traceability, supporting auditability and transparency requirements.

To meet the right-to-erasure demands, Prefect tasks can be designed to integrate with data management APIs to securely delete or anonymize personal data after task completion. For example, a Prefect flow can programmatically trigger data deletion routines compliant with GDPR retention schedules. Furthermore, the Prefect Cloud or Enterprise tier's role-based access control (RBAC) mechanisms ensure that data access during flow execution is restricted to authorized personnel, reducing risks of policy violations.

HIPAA compliance considerations focus on the protection of electronic protected health information (ePHI) within the U.S. healthcare domain. Compliance with HIPAA requires safeguarding confidentiality, integrity, and availability of ePHI, alongside strict access controls and audit capabilities.

Deploying Prefect in HIPAA-governed environments hinges on securing the workflow infrastructure and enforcing strict governance over data flows that handle ePHI. Prefect's configuration enables encrypted communication channels (TLS) between agents and servers, ensuring secure data transit. Additionally, Prefect's deployment on private cloud or on-premises infrastructures allows organizations to tightly control system access and data residency-both critical HIPAA criteria.

Prefect's event logging and monitoring features generate comprehensive audit trails for every flow and task execution. These audit logs are essential for HIPAA compliance validation and forensic analysis. Integration with authentication frameworks supporting multi-factor authentication (MFA) and single sign-on (SSO) further fortifies access protections within Prefect deployments.

Workflow designers must carefully segregate ePHI processing pipelines within Prefect flows and avoid unnecessary data replication. Techniques such as encryption at rest for intermediate data storage or persistent artifacts bolster data security during workflow transitions. Workflow state handlers can be customized to trigger alerts or remediation actions upon detection of anomalous behavior, helping maintain compliance with HIPAA's Security Rule.

SOC 2 alignment strategies define criteria for managing customer data based on five trust service principles: security, availability, processing integrity, confidentiality, and privacy. Organizations leveraging Prefect must engineer their data orchestration workflows to uphold these attributes and facilitate third-party SOC 2 audits.

Prefect's intrinsic architecture supports security by enabling fine-grained access controls and encrypting data in transit. Availability is enhanced through automated retry mechanisms, failure notifications, and scalable task execution-which helps meet system uptime requirements. Processing integrity is assured by deterministic flow executions with explicit state management, eliminating inconsistencies and undetected errors.

Confidentiality and privacy mandates are reinforced via integration with external key management systems for artifact encryption and access token protection. Prefect's extensible architecture allows embedding custom compliance checks or automated policy enforcement tasks within flows, providing continuous compliance monitoring.

To prepare for SOC 2 audits, organizations can leverage Prefect's comprehensive activity logs that document user actions, flow runs, and system events. Centralized logging paired with metrics collection enables evidence gathering for compliance reporting. Workflow provisioning and deployment automation tools can be employed to standardize infrastructure and software baselines, reducing risks relating to configuration drift-a common audit focus area.

Practical alignment strategies include:

- **Data Classification and Flow Segmentation:** Identify and classify data inputs and outputs managed by Prefect flows. Establish dedicated workflows for regulated data domains to isolate sensitive information and restrict access accordingly.

- **Access Controls and Identity Management:** Utilize Prefect's RBAC features combined with enterprise identity providers to enforce least-privilege access. Employ MFA and SSO integrations where possible to enhance authentication security.

- **Immutable Audit Trails:** Enable and retain detailed execution logs, metadata, and state transitions for all Prefect workflows. Regularly export these logs to secure, tamper-evident storage solutions to satisfy audit requirements.

- **Encryption and Data Protection:** Apply encryption for data at rest and in transit associated with Prefect tasks and artifacts. Automate key rotation policies and leverage hardware security modules (HSMs) where feasible.

- **Workflow Testing and Validation:** Implement rigorous testing pipelines that simulate compliance scenarios such as data deletion requests or access revocations. Use Prefect's parameterization and conditional branching to flexibly adapt flows for compliance events.

- **Incident Response and Monitoring:** Integrate Prefect monitoring systems with centralized security information and event management (SIEM) platforms. Automate alerts for anomalous activities or compliance breaches detected during flow execution.

- **Documentation and Continuous Improvement:** Maintain official documentation mapping Prefect roles, configurations, and workflow designs to specific compliance controls. Perform periodic reviews aligned with regulatory updates to refine processes dynamically.

A proactive approach combining Prefect's native orchestration capabilities with organizational governance policies achieves a resilient compliance posture. Continuous alignment efforts enable adaptation to evolving legal mandates without sacrificing operational scalability or agility. Ultimately, the fusion of well-architected data workflows with compliance frameworks empowers enterprises to safeguard sensitive data, uphold customer trust, and mitigate regulatory risks comprehensively.

7.5. Data Privacy in Workflow Orchestration

Workflow orchestration involves the coordinated execution of multiple interconnected tasks and services, often spanning heterogeneous environments and organizational boundaries. Such orchestration inherently processes vast volumes of data, including sensitive or personally identifiable information (PII). Protecting data privacy throughout the orchestration lifecycle is critical to maintaining compliance with regulatory frameworks such as GDPR, HIPAA, and CCPA, as well as preserving stakeholder trust. This necessitates a comprehensive strategy that addresses privacy at every stage: data ingestion, processing, storage, transmission, and archival.

A fundamental principle in privacy-centric orchestration is the *minimization of data exposure*. This starts by strictly limiting the scope of data accessed or exchanged between workflow components to the absolute minimum required to achieve their functional objectives. Data minimization can be enforced via fine-grained access control policies and data classification schemes that annotate each data element with its sensitivity level. By ensuring components receive only anonymized or pseudonymized inputs unless explicitly authorized, the attack surface for data leakage can be substantially reduced.

Privacy enforcement mechanisms must be embedded within the workflow orchestrator's core. These mechanisms include *policy-driven data governance* models where privacy policies— expressed in machine-readable languages such as XACML or PPL—dictate permitted data manipulations and flows. The orchestrator evaluates these policies dynamically as workflows proceed, preventing unauthorized data access or transmission in real time. Policy enforcement points integrated at data ingress, egress, and inter-task communication further strengthen the guarantee that privacy constraints are invariantly respected.

Another essential technique to embed in workflow design is *privacy-preserving computation.* Methods such as secure multiparty computation (SMPC), homomorphic encryption, and differential privacy can enable processing on sensitive data without exposing it in plaintext. For instance, homomorphic encryption allows arithmetic operations directly over encrypted datasets, thereby enabling analytics or decision-making within the workflow without decrypting data. Implementing such cryptographic primitives in orchestration highlights a shift from traditional plaintext workflows toward *privacy-by-design* paradigms.

Isolation and sandboxing of workflow tasks contribute significantly to privacy preservation. Containerization and virtualized execution environments restrict data leakage by limiting the runtime context and ensuring that any residual data is securely erased post-execution. Combined with robust auditing and provenance tracking, these measures help detect and prevent unauthorized data access or misuse during orchestrated executions.

Data transmission between workflow components, often distributed across cloud and edge systems, presents substantial privacy risks. End-to-end encryption protocols such as TLS must be mandatorily employed to secure data in transit. Additionally, implementing secure channels with mutual authentication and key management frameworks prevents man-in-the-middle attacks and unauthorized interception. For latency-sensitive workflows, lightweight cryptographic protocols with minimal computational overhead may be selected to balance performance and privacy.

At the storage layer, encryption of data at rest using strong, standardized cryptographic algorithms is indispensable. Key management systems must be integrated tightly with the orchestrator to ensure encryption keys are protected and accessible only to authorized processes. Data retention policies derived from privacy regulations should enforce timely data destruction or anonymization, which can be orchestrated as dedicated workflow steps to maintain end-to-end control over sensitive data lifecycle.

Embedding differential privacy into data analytics workflows offers mathematical guarantees that individual data subjects cannot be re-identified from aggregate outputs. Adding controlled random noise to query results or training datasets can thwart inference attacks while preserving statistical utility. Such techniques can be orchestrated transparently as modular workflow components, enabling privacy guarantees to be composable with existing data transformation pipelines.

Lastly, workflow orchestration platforms must incorporate comprehensive *privacy auditing and monitoring* capabilities. Continuous logging of data access, transformation, transfer events, and policy decisions provides an immutable provenance record critical for compliance verification and forensic analysis. These logs must also be protected against tampering and unauthorized access, ensuring the integrity and confidentiality of privacy audit trails.

Safeguarding data privacy within workflow orchestration demands a multifaceted approach that minimizes unnecessary data exposure, enforces rigorous privacy policies, and integrates advanced privacy-preserving techniques directly into execution environments. Redesigning workflows with privacy-by-design principles and leveraging state-of-the-art cryptographic tools not only mitigates risks of data breaches but also strengthens regulatory compliance and user trust in complex, data-driven orchestrated systems.

7.6. Vulnerability Management and Security Updates

Robust vulnerability management is critical to maintaining the security posture of an orchestration system. Given the complexity and dynamic nature of orchestration platforms such as Kubernetes or Docker Swarm, the attack surface expands beyond the core orchestration software to include dependencies, container images, and underlying infrastructure components. Effective vulnerability management involves systematic identification, assessment, remediation, and continuous monitoring of security risks associated with software components.

Managing software dependencies begins with a comprehensive inventory of all components in the orchestration stack. This includes the orchestration engine itself, container runtime, network plugins, storage drivers, and any auxiliary tools or libraries. Automated dependency scanning tools integrate with CI/CD pipelines to analyze manifests, Dockerfiles, and Helm charts, flagging known vulnerabilities using vulnerability databases such as the National Vulnerability Database (NVD) or vendor-specific advisories. Container image scanning is equally crucial; images must be scanned both at build time and during runtime deployment to identify outdated packages or insecure configurations.

Monitoring threats to an orchestration system requires both static and dynamic security assessments. Static analysis leverages vulnerability scanning tools to examine source code and configuration files for potential misconfigurations and insecure coding patterns. Dynamic monitoring involves real-time anomaly detection and behavioral analysis of orchestration activities and workloads. Threat intelligence feeds enrich the context by providing updated indicators of compromise (IOCs) relevant to the orchestration ecosystem. Integration with Security Information and Event Management (SIEM) systems enables correlation and prioritization of security events stemming from orchestration components.

Systematic application of security patches and updates is a fundamental defense strategy but must be balanced against operational continuity and stability. The orchestration environment should enforce strict version control and maintain a staging environment that mirrors production to validate patches before deployment. Updating the orchestration system and associated components should follow a well-defined change management process that includes testing for compatibility, automated rollback mechanisms, and downtime minimization strategies such as rolling updates or blue–green deployments.

Algorithm 1 Structured Vulnerability Management for Orchestration Systems

---

1: **procedure** ManageVulnerabilities
2:     Inventory all components and dependencies
3:     Schedule regular automated vulnerability scans on:

- Container images

- Orchestration binaries

- Configuration files

- Third-party libraries

4:     Integrate threat intelligence feeds for up-to-date vulnerability data
5:     Monitor event logs and orchestration activity for anomalies
6:     **if** vulnerabilities detected **then**
7:         Classify based on severity and exploitability
8:         Prioritize remediation steps accordingly
9:         Test patches in a staging environment
10:         Apply validated patches to production with a rollback plan
11:         Document changes and update the inventory
12:     **end if**
13:     Continuously repeat this process at defined intervals
14: **end procedure**

Automation plays a pivotal role, as vulnerability scanning tools such as Clair, Trivy, or Anchore can be integrated into the continuous delivery pipeline to enforce policies that prevent deployment of vulnerable artifacts. Likewise, orchestrators often provide APIs or operators facilitating automated patch management and reporting.

Managing third-party dependencies requires vigilance given their frequent updates and the introduction of new vulnerabilities. Dependency management tools such as Dependabot or Renovate automate pull requests for dependency updates, ensuring maintainers are promptly aware of required upgrades. It is crucial to combine automated tools with human oversight to verify that updates do not introduce regressions or conflicts within the orchestration environment.

Patch management for underlying operating systems and container hosts is equally essential. Tools like Ansible, Puppet, or Chef can orchestrate patch deployment across clusters in a controlled manner. Kernel and system library updates must be scheduled and validated regularly, as attackers frequently exploit outdated system components to gain persistence or privilege escalation inside workloads.

Zero-day vulnerabilities-those newly discovered and not yet patched-require proactive mitigation techniques until official patches become available. These may include implementing network segmentation to limit lateral movement, applying runtime security policies such as Kubernetes Pod Security Policies (PSPs) or Open Policy Agent (OPA) constraints, and employing intrusion detection and prevention systems (IDS/IPS) tailored for containerized environments.

Audit logging and vulnerability reporting are essential components of a mature vulnerability management process. Logs from orchestration components and scanners should be centrally aggregated and analyzed to measure the effectiveness of remediation efforts and compliance with organizational security standards. Mapping metrics such as Mean Time to Detection (MTTD) and Mean Time to Remediation (MTTR) enables continuous improvement of the security operations workflow.

Maintaining a secure and up-to-date orchestration system mandates an integrated approach combining comprehensive dependency management, continuous scanning, threat monitoring, and disciplined patch application. The fusion of automation with human expertise ensures resilience against evolving security threats that target the complex, multi-layered orchestration ecosystem.

Chapter 8

Operational Excellence and Observability at Scale

Running workflows in development is one thing—ensuring their health, performance, and rapid evolution in production is another. This chapter provides a deep dive into the operational principles and observability tools that empower teams to deliver reliable data pipelines, maintain cost efficiency, and drive continuous improvement, even as scale and complexity increase.

8.1. Monitoring and Alerting for Production Workflows

Robust monitoring and alerting mechanisms are indispensable for ensuring the reliability and performance of production-grade Prefect workflows. By seamlessly integrating Prefect with widely adopted observability tools such as Prometheus and Grafana, organizations can achieve comprehensive visibility, enabling rapid detection and mitigation of issues before they adversely affect critical business functions.

Prefect emits a wide range of telemetry data, including workflow run states, task-level metrics, execution durations, and failure events, which form the foundation for an effective monitoring framework. To leverage this data, the first step involves configuring Prefect's telemetry exporters to expose relevant metrics in a format consumable by Prometheus. This typically requires deploying Prefect's API and Orion server alongside Prometheus exporters capable of scraping metrics endpoints exposed on HTTP.

The integration starts with enabling Prometheus metrics in Prefect's deployment configuration. Prefect's Orion service incorporates a metrics endpoint (usually accessible at /metrics) that adheres to the Prometheus exposition format. This endpoint can be enabled by setting the environment variable:

```
PREFECT_API_METRICS_ENABLED=true
```

Once enabled, Prometheus is configured with a scrape_config tailored to the Prefect metrics endpoint:

```
scrape_configs:
  - job_name: 'prefect_workflows'
    static_configs:
      - targets: ['<PREFECT_SERVER_HOST>:4200']
```

This minimal setup ensures Prometheus periodically queries the Prefect metrics endpoint, aggregating key performance indicators such as task success rates, retry counts, and execution latencies.

With the telemetry pipeline established, visualization and dashboarding become critical to convert metrics into actionable insights. Grafana offers a powerful platform for creating dynamic dashboards visualizing Prefect workflow health over time. Users can construct panels showcasing aggregated task durations, workflow throughput, and failure trends. By leveraging Grafana's alerting engine, precise threshold-based or anomaly-detection alerts can be orchestrated to maintain vigilance over workflow behavior.

To enable proactive incident response, alerting rules in Grafana or Prometheus Alertmanager are carefully defined on key metrics indicative of operational anomalies. For example, alerts on sustained task failure rates exceeding a predefined threshold can signal emergent issues such as environmental misconfigurations or data quality regressions. A representative Prometheus alert rule might appear as:

```
groups:
- name: prefect_alerts
  rules:
  - alert: HighTaskFailureRate
    expr: increase(prefect_task_failures[10m]) / increase(
    prefect_task_runs[10m]) > 0.1
    for: 5m
    labels:
       severity: critical
    annotations:
       summary: "Task failure rate above 10% in the last 10
    minutes"
       description: "Prefect workflows have experienced a high
    failure rate indicative of potentially systemic issues."
```

This rule triggers an alert if more than 10% of task runs fail within a rolling 10-minute window, sustained for at least 5 minutes. Coupled with automated notification channels such as email, Slack, or PagerDuty, the alert system enables operations teams to undertake rapid remediation.

Beyond task failure rates, additional metrics and events are relevant for comprehensive monitoring, including:

- **Workflow run latency:** Detecting workflow executions exceeding expected durations.

- **Task retries:** Monitoring an abnormal increase in retries which may signal transient failures.

- **Orphaned or stuck flows:** Identifying workflows that remain in queued or running states beyond typical execution windows.

- **Resource utilization:** CPU, memory, and I/O metrics of Prefect agents and related infrastructure.

Integrating these metrics with correlated system-level observability provides a holistic perspective, enabling root cause analysis when bottlenecks or failures arise.

To facilitate efficient configuration management, modern infrastructures often employ declarative manifests and GitOps workflows to define monitoring and alerting configurations as code. This practice enhances reproducibility, auditability, and simplifies updates as workflow complexity evolves.

Lastly, it is prudent to incorporate synthetic monitoring or canary workflows that periodically simulate critical data pipelines under controlled conditions. Such synthetic tests act as early warning systems, detecting breaking changes or regressions caused by infrastructure shifts, dependency updates, or data anomalies.

Embedding Prefect workflows into a contemporary observability ecosystem centered on Prometheus and Grafana is fundamental for operational excellence. By combining real-time telemetry, insightful dashboards, and proactive alerting, organizations can achieve resilient orchestration environments that safeguard business continuity and accelerate incident response for diverse production workloads.

8.2. Cost Management and Resource Optimization

Effective cost management and resource optimization are critical components for maintaining scalable and sustainable workflows within Prefect environments. As organizations scale their automation and data orchestration capabilities, unchecked resource consumption can lead to escalating operational expenses. This section

194

outlines methodologies for tracking and analyzing workflow costs, right-sizing computational resources, and enforcing policies that balance performance requirements with budgetary constraints.

Tracking and Analyzing Workflow Costs

Precise visibility into resource utilization is the foundation of cost control. Prefect's architecture enables detailed metrics collection at multiple levels, including task execution time, compute resource allocation, and data transfer volumes. To gain actionable insights, these metrics must be aggregated and correlated with cost data obtained from underlying cloud providers or on-premises infrastructure.

A recommended approach is to integrate Prefect's telemetry with cost management tools that ingest usage logs and pricing models, such as AWS Cost Explorer or custom analytics dashboards. Prefect's metadata tags and labels can be leveraged to categorize workflows by project, environment, or priority, facilitating granular cost attribution. By analyzing trends and anomaly detection in resource consumption, teams can proactively identify inefficiencies or runaway workflows.

Right-Sizing Infrastructure

Selecting the appropriate infrastructure size is fundamental to optimizing costs in Prefect deployments. Over-provisioning leads to idle resources and wasted expenditure, whereas under-provisioning risks performance degradation and workflow failures. Right-sizing encompasses choosing virtual machine types, container limits, and executor parallelism settings that align with workload characteristics.

Profiling typical task resource requirements—CPU, memory, I/O— and their variance across runs informs this process. Prefect's task run history and execution logs provide empirical data for estimating resource footprints. Automated horizontal scaling mechanisms, such as Kubernetes Horizontal Pod Autoscalers (HPA), can dynamically adjust the number of Prefect Agents or task executors based on real-time demand, optimizing resource allocation in bursty or unpredictable workloads.

Additionally, adopting spot instances or preemptible VMs for non-critical or retryable tasks reduces expenses, albeit with the consideration of volatility and potential interruptions. Prefect's fault-tolerant and checkpointing features support such strategies by enabling task restarts without data loss.

Monitoring Resource Usage

Continuous monitoring is essential for maintaining an efficient resource consumption profile over time. Prefect's observability stack, combined with external monitoring tools such as Prometheus and Grafana, provides real-time dashboards and alerts on parameters like CPU utilization, memory allocation, queue lengths, and task failure rates.

Setting threshold-based alarms helps detect wasteful or abnormal resource use, triggering automated remediation workflows or human notifications. Correlating these monitoring signals with cost metrics enables teams to prioritize optimization efforts effectively and justifies investments in infrastructure upgrades or software improvements.

Logging standardized resource usage metadata directly within Prefect task runs simplifies auditability and post-mortem cost analysis, enabling precise identification of high-cost contributors.

Implementing Cost-Control Policies

Robust cost governance relies on enforceable policies embedded within the Prefect orchestration framework. These policies serve to constrain resource consumption, mandate efficiency standards, and prevent runaway costs.

At the workflow definition level, resource limits can be specified for individual tasks or flows, capping CPU and memory usage to prevent oversubscription. Prefect supports setting task timeouts and concurrency limits, reducing the risk of long-running or duplicate executions inflating costs.

Policy-driven scheduling can prioritize critical workflows during peak periods and defer less urgent tasks to off-peak times when resources are cheaper. Rate limiting external API calls or database queries within tasks also preserves quotas and avoids external penalties.

In larger organizations, role-based access control (RBAC) integrated with Prefect Cloud or Server restricts who can deploy or scale workflows, minimizing cost risks associated with uncontrolled environment changes.

Case Study: Scalable Prefect Deployment Cost Optimization

Consider an enterprise migrating multiple ETL pipelines to Prefect Cloud, initially experiencing inflated costs due to indiscriminate task concurrency and oversized VM instances. By applying the techniques above, the team first instrumented detailed task telemetry and linked it with AWS cost reports. Analysis revealed that certain tasks consumed memory disproportionately without proportional performance gains.

The team adjusted container resource requests and limits, enforcing memory ceilings and gradually tuning CPU shares. Kubernetes HPAs were configured to scale Prefect Agents based on queue length metrics, reducing always-on instances. Expensive on-demand instances were replaced with a hybrid spot/on-demand cluster, leveraging Prefect's retries to handle spot interruptions gracefully.

Monitoring was enhanced with Grafana dashboards tracking cost-related KPIs and alerting on anomaly spikes. The final cost-control policy mandated resource quotas for new workflows and limited concurrent executions per team.

These measures yielded a 40% reduction in infrastructure costs within two billing cycles while maintaining SLA compliance, illustrating the effectiveness of comprehensive cost management and resource optimization strategies.

Summary of Best Practices

- **Instrument and integrate:** Collect detailed execution and resource usage metrics and integrate them with cost management platforms.

- **Profile workloads:** Analyze historical task resource consumption to inform accurate infrastructure sizing decisions.

- **Leverage autoscaling:** Use dynamic scaling capabilities to adjust resource allocation to demand patterns.

- **Monitor continuously:** Establish real-time observability with alerts tied to resource and cost anomalies.

- **Enforce policies:** Configure limits, quotas, and scheduling priorities to prevent cost overruns.

- **Balance cost and reliability:** Employ spot instances thoughtfully, utilizing Prefect's fault tolerance features to mitigate interruptions.

Adopting these techniques empowers organizations to exert fine-grained control over Prefect environment costs, enabling workflows that are both performant and economically sustainable at scale.

8.3. Incident Response and Remediation

Effective incident response in production environments hinges on the development and implementation of robust playbooks combined with automation tools that facilitate rapid diagnostics and remediation. Playbooks codify the operational knowledge necessary to systematically address incidents, while automation reduces human error and expedites resolution times. Together, these elements form the backbone for minimizing downtime and preserving service integrity under adverse conditions.

A comprehensive incident response playbook should begin by defining incident classification criteria, mapping symptoms to severity levels and impacted services. This classification streamlines prioritization and resource allocation during high-pressure scenarios. Following classification, the playbook prescribes clear, stepwise diagnostic procedures to identify root causes, leveraging real-time telemetry data such as logs, metrics, and traces. Modern observability platforms provide APIs for automated retrieval and correlation of these data sources, enabling swift contextualization of incidents.

The diagnostic phase benefits greatly from real-time automation scripts that perform initial health checks and anomaly detection. For instance, a script might validate connectivity to critical databases, confirm the integrity of configuration files, or compare recent deployment versions against known stable releases. Automating these standard tests accelerates baseline assessments and often surfaces the cause without human intervention.

To illustrate, consider the following simplified example of an automated diagnostic script in Python using Prometheus's HTTP API to check service health metrics:

```python
import requests
import time

PROMETHEUS_URL = 'http://prometheus.example.com/api/v1/query'
QUERY = 'up{job="backend-service"}'

def check_service_health():
    response = requests.get(PROMETHEUS_URL, params={'query':
    QUERY})
    result = response.json()['data']['result']
    for metric in result:
        instance = metric['metric']['instance']
```

199

```
status = int(metric['value'][1])
if status != 1:
    print(f'Service on {instance} is down')
else:
    print(f'Service on {instance} is up')

if __name__ == '__main__':
    while True:
        check_service_health()
        time.sleep(60)
```

This script queries the up metric to verify the availability of each backend service instance every minute, enabling early detection of partial outages.

Following diagnosis, the playbook should delineate remediation steps, carefully balancing automated corrective actions with guided human interventions. Automated remediation may encompass restarting failed services, rolling back unstable deployments, or adjusting resource allocations dynamically. Safeguards such as canary releases, circuit breakers, and rate limiting are often integrated as preventive measures within the automation logic to reduce incident impact.

A typical remediation automation flow might involve logic such as the following:

```
if service_health_check_fails:
    attempt automated restart of service
    if restart_unsuccessful after 3 tries:
        trigger alert for manual investigation
else:
    continue monitoring
```

This approach ensures that automated procedures handle transient faults autonomously while escalating persistent issues to engineers promptly.

The implementation of systematic remediation strategies requires integration with deployment pipelines and orchestration platforms. Infrastructure as Code (IaC) tools facilitate rapid environmental recovery by enabling version-controlled rollback and consistent configuration redeployment. For example, associating incident playbook steps with specific IaC scripts leads to repeatable remediation exercises that reduce human error and enforce operational best practices.

Real-time diagnostics and remediation also benefit from incident triaging dashboards that aggregate alerts, diagnostics outputs, and remediation progress. Visualization aids like heatmaps, timeline charts, and dependency graphs provide operators with actionable situational awareness, allowing faster correlation of events and root cause isolation.

Automation must be designed with extensibility and safety in mind. Key principles include:

- **Idempotency:** Remediation actions should be repeatable without unintended side effects.

- **Rollback capability:** Automated changes should include mechanisms for reversal in case of failure.

- **Auditability:** All automated and manual steps must be logged thoroughly for compliance and postincident analyses.

- **Human-in-the-loop:** Critical or destructive operations require explicit human approval or intervention.

Moreover, playbooks must be living documents, continuously refined through postmortem reviews and operational feedback. Incident response drills and chaos engineering experiments simulate failures to validate and improve automated workflows and team readiness.

Integrating robust incident playbooks with automation tools transforms incident response from a reactive firefighting effort to a proactive, controlled process. Real-time diagnostics with automated health checks enable rapid fault detection, while systematic remediation reduces mean time to recovery (MTTR) and preserves service continuity. The combination of codified knowledge, automation, and monitoring visualization forms a resilient framework essential for managing complex production environments at scale.

8.4. Flow Documentation and Knowledge Management

Effective management of workflow operations hinges on robust documentation and comprehensive lifecycle management of flows. Across complex systems, ensuring that flow artifacts are both accessible and maintainable reduces operational friction and accelerates onboarding processes. This section explores critical practices for creating searchable documentation, implementing version control, and fostering collaborative knowledge sharing, thereby enabling streamlined workflow operations.

Central to managing flows is the establishment of well-organized, machine-readable, and human-readable documentation. Documenting each flow's purpose, triggers, data inputs and outputs, processing logic, dependencies, and expected behaviors creates a single source of truth that minimizes ambiguity. Employing standardized metadata tags within documentation facilitates indexing and searchability, critical in environments with extensive flow repositories.

Metadata fields should include:

- **Flow Name and Identifier**: Unique and descriptive identifiers.

- **Version Number**: Indicating evolution stages.

- **Author and Ownership**: Clarifying responsibility.

- **Creation and Modification Dates**: Enabling historical analysis.

- **Dependencies and Related Resources**: Documenting upstream and downstream connections.

- **Functional Description**: Summarizing the business process or technical operation executed by the flow.

Incorporating structured documentation formats such as Markdown enhanced with YAML front matter or JSON-LD enables seamless parsing by automated tools and integration into documentation portals. Additionally, linking to external design diagrams or related code repositories enriches contextual understanding.

Controlling the lifecycle of flows requires rigorous application of version control systems (VCS) traditionally reserved for software code. Each flow artifact—configuration files, automation scripts, or accompanying documentation—should be checked into a centralized VCS such as Git. This approach supports branching, merging, and rollback capabilities essential in collaborative teams managing frequent changes.

Lifecycle stages of flows typically encompass:

- **Development**: Creation and initial testing.

- **Staging**: Deployment in a pre-production environment for validation.

- **Production**: Operational use.

- **Deprecation and Archival**: Phasing out obsolete or replaced flows while preserving their history.

Tracking changes via commit messages, tags, and pull requests creates an auditable trail that enhances traceability and accountability. Integrating continuous integration/continuous deployment (CI/CD) pipelines automates the promotion of flows across these lifecycle stages, enforcing quality gates and ensuring consistency.

```
# Clone the repository
git clone https://example.com/flows.git

# Create and switch to new branch for feature development
git checkout -b feature/flow-improvement

# Stage and commit changes
git add flow_definition.yaml
git commit -m "Refactor flow to improve error handling"

# Push branch to remote repository
git push origin feature/flow-improvement

# Open Pull Request for review and merge
```

Facilitating cross-functional collaboration requires that flow documentation and knowledge be broadly accessible and participatory. Centralized knowledge bases or internal wikis populated with indexed flow documentation allow users to discover relevant flows through keyword search and contextual filtering. Embedding examples, troubleshooting guides, and best practice recommendations within these resources lowers the barrier to entry for new users and heightens operational resilience.

Communication platforms integrated with flow management tools enable real-time discussions on flow design, defects, or enhancement proposals. Leveraging annotation capabilities directly within flow diagrams or configuration files fosters context-rich conversations that improve clarity and decision-making.

Formalizing review cycles, such as periodic documentation audits and knowledge-sharing sessions, ensures documentation remains current and useful. Organizations should cultivate an ownership culture where both developers and users are responsible for contributing updates and corrections to documentation. This collective maintenance mitigates information decay which otherwise undermines operational efficiency.

Selecting appropriate tooling infrastructure accelerates adoption and maintains the integrity of flow documentation and lifecycle management. Platforms supporting integrated version control, searchable catalogs, and collaboration features reduce friction in knowledge exchange. Examples include:

- **Documentation Generators**: Tools that auto-generate flow documentation from annotations or metadata embedded in source definitions.

- **Flow Repositories**: Specialized registries with built-in search and dependency management.

- **CI/CD Integrations**: Automating deployments alongside documentation updates ensures synchronization.

- **ChatOps**: Leveraging chatbots that retrieve flow status or documentation snippets in response to queries.

Automated validation of documentation completeness and consistency against flow definitions can trigger alerts when documentation drifts from actual flow configurations. Such automation enforces discipline and protects the value of knowledge assets over time.

The cumulative effect of rigorous flow documentation, disciplined version control, and collaborative knowledge practices manifests in significant operational improvements. Troubleshooting is expedited when accurate flow information is readily available, avoiding costly delays due to knowledge gaps. Onboarding new engineers and operators becomes efficient as they gain rapid insight into system behaviors without prolonged shadowing or guesswork.

Moreover, lifecycle-managed flows reduce risks associated with ad hoc changes or undocumented modifications, thereby enhancing system stability and compliance posture. As organizations scale, these practices establish a resilient foundation for continuous improvement and innovation in workflow automation.

Embedding thorough documentation and knowledge management

into flow operations transforms an otherwise opaque and error-prone process into a transparent, controllable, and scalable discipline. This discipline underpins agile, reliable, and effective workflow ecosystems critical to modern enterprise demands.

8.5. Case Studies: Managing Large-Scale Flows

The operationalization of large-scale data workflows introduces complexities that grow nonlinearly with the volume, variety, and velocity of data, as well as the number of interdependent tasks and teams involved. Prefect, as a modern workflow orchestration platform, offers a robust foundation for managing these complexities. This section examines several illustrative case studies from organizations that have successfully employed Prefect to orchestrate critical, high-throughput processes. Analysis of their approaches exposes key success factors, common pitfalls, and practical strategies essential for managing workflows at scale.

Case Study 1: Financial Services Firm — Real-Time Risk Analytics Pipeline

A multinational financial services company leveraged Prefect to automate its real-time risk analytics pipeline, which ingests market data from multiple sources, processes it with complex algorithms, and produces actionable risk metrics every few minutes. The pipeline consists of hundreds of tasks distributed across data ingestion, transformation, model scoring, and reporting modules.

Key to their success was Prefect's flexible dependency management and dynamic mapping functionality to parallelize workloads. By composing task groups with clear upstream/downstream relationships and using parameterized flow runs, the team could run numerous independent risk models concurrently while maintaining reliable end-to-end orchestration. Prefect's state handlers and event hooks allowed early detection of anomalies and enabled automatic retries with exponential backoff for transient failures, reducing manual intervention.

Operational insights included the necessity of granular task segmentation: splitting large monolithic tasks into smaller, idempotent units improved error isolation and accelerated failure recovery. Additionally, adopting Prefect's centralized UI enabled real-time monitoring and post-mortem analyses, which were critical for compliance and auditing requirements.

Recurring challenges encompassed managing resource contention within a constrained Kubernetes cluster infrastructure and tuning task concurrency limits to avoid cascading failures. The team found that integrating resource-aware scheduling, combined with Prefect's concurrency controls, stabilized throughput without overwhelming downstream services.

Case Study 2: E-Commerce Platform — End-to-End Data Engineering Workflows

An established e-commerce platform used Prefect to orchestrate its data engineering workflows responsible for customer behavior analytics, inventory forecasting, and promotional campaign targeting. These workflows run on a daily schedule, comprising thousands of tasks that process batch data from distributed transactional and event stores.

The organization prioritized reproducibility and data quality. Implementing strict schema validation and data freshness checks within Prefect tasks ensured that only trusted datasets propagated downstream. Prefect's parameterized flows and integration with version-controlled script repositories enabled versioned deployment of workflows synchronized with CI/CD pipelines, fostering consistent environments across development, staging, and production.

Fail-over scenarios, such as upstream data source delays or partial failures, were mitigated through Prefect's conditional task triggering and dynamic rerun capabilities. For example, failed data extraction tasks triggered alerting workflows and prevented subsequent transformations, avoiding the propagation of corrupted data.

Key lessons included the importance of comprehensive metadata tagging within flows and tasks to facilitate lineage tracking and impact analysis. Prefect's metadata extension points were adapted to capture rich annotations, improving root cause diagnostics during incidents.

The organization encountered challenges in orchestrating heterogeneous compute environments, including hybrid clouds and on-premises clusters. Employing Prefect agents with custom execution environments helped abstract underlying infrastructure differences, providing a unified control plane for workflow execution.

Case Study 3: Biotechnology Research Consortium — Large-Scale Genomic Data Processing

A consortium of biotechnology research institutions implemented Prefect to coordinate their genomic data processing pipelines, which involve complex bioinformatics workflows spanning multiple stages such as raw sequence alignment, variant calling, and annotation. Each workflow processes terabytes of data and can comprise thousands of thousands of parallel tasks per run.

Prefect's dynamic task mapping enabled fine-grained parallelism, spawning independent tasks per sequence batch without excessive upfront task definition. The team leveraged Prefect's result caching and conditional execution features to prevent redundant recalculations, saving considerable computational resources. By integrating Prefect with Kubernetes custom resource definitions, they achieved elastic scaling of underlying compute nodes triggered by workflow demand.

Critical to their operation was the enforcement of strict provenance and traceability for scientific reproducibility. Prefect's rich logging framework and API-driven metadata capture facilitated comprehensive documentation of workflow executions, ensuring transparency and repeatability for downstream analysis.

Common challenges arose from the need to synchronize workflows across multiple institutional boundaries, each with distinct security policies and data access controls. To address this, Prefect's extensible authentication and secrets management features were incorporated, enabling secure credential rotation and cross-organization access without compromising compliance.

Cross-Cutting Insights and Best Practices

From these distinct domains and operational contexts, several overarching principles emerge for effectively managing large-scale flows with Prefect:

- **Modular Flow Design:** Decomposing workflows into small, atomic tasks enhances fault isolation, increases parallelism, and improves maintainability. Prefect's API supports modular task and flow construction, encouraging reuse and clear dependency articulation.

- **Dynamic and Parameterized Execution:** Leveraging Prefect's dynamic mapping and flow parameterization enables pipelines to adapt fluidly to varying data sizes and external conditions, optimizing resource utilization and throughput.

- **Observability and Alerting:** Comprehensive visibility into task states, execution metrics, and logs is indispensable. Prefect's UI and API facilitate near real-time monitoring coupled with customizable notification handlers to promptly surface anomalies.

- **Resilience and Automated Recovery:** Automated retry policies, exponential backoff strategies, and conditional task restarts dramatically reduce downtime and manual intervention in error scenarios.

- **Integration with Infrastructure and Security:** Seamless compatibility with container orchestration platforms, CI/CD systems, and secure secrets management underpins operational robustness and compliance adherence.

- **Metadata and Provenance Capture:** Embedding rich contextual information throughout workflow execution supports auditability and simplifies debugging.

Addressing challenges related to resource contention, heterogeneous execution environments, and multi-tenant orchestration platforms often necessitates extending Prefect's native capabilities with custom agents, resource-aware scheduling policies, or integration with third-party workflow governance tools.

Technical Illustration: Implementing Dynamic Task Mapping for Parallel Processing

The following example demonstrates a simplified pattern derived from the case studies to orchestrate batch processing over a variable list of inputs, enhancing scalability and fault tolerance.

```
from prefect import flow, task

@task(retries=3, retry_delay_seconds=10)
def process_item(item):
    # Placeholder for complex processing logic
    result = item ** 2
    return result

@flow
def batch_processing_flow(items: list[int]):
    results = process_item.map(items)
    return results

if __name__ == "__main__":
    input_data = list(range(1000))  # Large-scale input set
    output = batch_processing_flow(input_data)
    print(output)
```

```
[0, 1, 4, 9, 16, ..., 998001]
```

This pattern adapts naturally as the input data size scales, with Prefect managing task scheduling, retries, and state management transparently. Such scalable compositions underpin the orchestration strategies in the reviewed case studies.

These concrete examples demonstrate Prefect's adaptability and robustness in managing critical workflows at scale, offering valuable operational lessons to practitioners striving to tame complexity in distributed data ecosystems.

8.6. Continuous Improvement and Workflow Review Processes

Sustainable feedback loops are fundamental to achieving operational excellence in complex orchestration systems. These feedback mechanisms enable the identification of inefficiencies, the validation of changes, and the adaptation of workflows in response to evolving requirements and environmental factors. Effective implementation entails three interdependent components: structured workflow reviews, metric-driven evolution, and regular retrospectives.

Workflow reviews serve as systematic checkpoints during which existing processes and orchestration strategies are evaluated against predetermined performance criteria. These assessments should be scheduled at regular intervals and triggered by significant operational events such as system upgrades, major incidents, or integration of new components. The objective is twofold: detect bottlenecks and verify alignment with business objectives. Often structured as review meetings involving cross-functional stakeholders, these sessions utilize detailed process maps, execution logs, and key performance indicators (KPIs) to provide comprehensive visibility into operational status.

Metric-driven evolution is a cornerstone of objective decision-making within continuous improvement frameworks. Rather than relying on qualitative assessments alone, organizations must identify a robust set of quantitative metrics that reflect orchestration health and efficiency. Commonly monitored parameters include pipeline throughput, error rates, latency distributions, resource utilization, and compliance adherence. Continuous monitoring systems should automate the collection and aggregation of these metrics, enabling real-time dashboards and historical trend analyses. The interpretation of these metrics guides prioritized adjustments to the orchestration workflows, permitting incremental and focused evolution. Algorithmic techniques such as statistical process control and anomaly detection further enhance the ability to discern meaningful variations from baseline operational noise.

Retrospectives represent deliberate, reflective gatherings where the operational team collectively examines recent orchestration cycles to extract lessons learned. These sessions emphasize transparency and psychological safety, encouraging candid discussion of successes and failures. Retrospectives focus on the interplay of human factors, tooling effectiveness, and procedural adequacy. Structured formats, such as the Start-Stop-Continue method or the Five Whys root-cause analysis, facilitate systematic exploration of issues and opportunities. Outcomes typically include actionable improvement items, assigned responsibilities, and agreed timelines, which are then integrated into subsequent workflow review agendas and metric frameworks.

Integration of these components into a closed-loop system produces a resilient and adaptive orchestration environment. Figure illustrates this cyclical process, wherein data-driven insights from monitoring feed into workflow reviews, which in turn inform retrospective discussions, subsequently giving rise to refined orchestration designs and configurations.

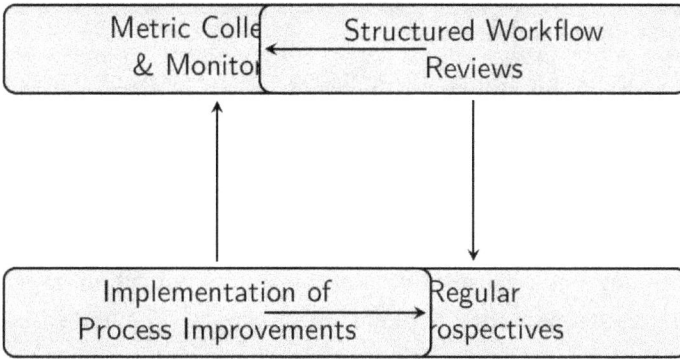

The robustness of these feedback loops depends on consistent data integrity and the cultural mandate to prioritize continuous learning. Organizations are encouraged to invest in instrumentation that captures fine-grained event data, enabling root-cause triangulation during workflow reviews. Additionally, governance structures must empower cross-disciplinary participation and the time allocation necessary for meaningful retrospectives.

In practice, achieving sustainable feedback loops necessitates tailoring the review cadence and metric selection to the organization's operational tempo, domain complexity, and risk profile. For high-frequency deployment pipelines, daily or weekly mini-reviews combined with automated alerts for KPI deviations offer timely insights. Conversely, slower-changing environments may adopt monthly or quarterly cycles. Likewise, metric sets evolve over time; initial focus on availability and error rates may expand to include user experience scores, cost efficiency, and security compliance metrics.

Explicit documentation of workflow changes and retrospective outcomes ensures knowledge continuity and accountability throughout the orchestration lifecycle. Version-controlled repositories of process documentation and tooling configurations complement

213

these efforts by enabling traceability of improvements and facilitating rollback if necessary.

To exemplify an automated metric-driven evolution, consider a scenario where pipeline latency consistently exceeds threshold values during peak usage. Automated monitoring alerts trigger a workflow review involving infrastructure and development teams. Analysis reveals suboptimal resource allocation in concurrent job scheduling. A retrospective identifies communication gaps between teams regarding deployment priorities. The agreed-upon improvement involves modifying the orchestration scheduler to incorporate dynamic scaling policies and enhanced communication protocols. Upon implementation, monitoring confirms latency reduction, validating the effectiveness of the feedback loop.

The virtuous cycle of continuous improvement not only optimizes orchestration performance but also cultivates organizational agility, fostering responsiveness to technological advances and shifting business landscapes. This iterative refinement paradigm is indispensable for maintaining competitive advantage in rapidly evolving digital ecosystems.

Chapter 9

Future Directions: Prefect and the Evolution of Orchestration

What does the future hold for workflow orchestration as data architectures, technology, and user demands continue to evolve? This chapter looks forward, uncovering disruptive trends, community innovations, and emerging paradigms that will shape Prefect and orchestration platforms for years to come. Gain foresight into how your workflows can stay ahead of the curve in a rapidly changing landscape.

9.1. Serverless and Edge Orchestration

The evolution of computational paradigms has witnessed serverless and edge computing emerge as transformative approaches in workflow orchestration, fundamentally reshaping how distributed applications are deployed and managed. These paradigms decouple the concerns of infrastructure provisioning from business logic execution, enabling the development of ultra-scalable, responsive, and cost-efficient systems in increasingly decentralized environments.

Serverless computing introduces an abstraction layer where developers author functions or discrete units of computation without the need to manage the underlying server infrastructure. Cloud providers automatically scale and schedule execution based on demand, with billing granularly tied to actual compute time and resource utilization. Within workflow orchestration, serverless execution enables dynamic, event-driven pipelines that can elastically expand or contract, eliminating idle capacity and reducing operational overhead. This model is particularly effective for workloads characterized by intermittent bursts or fine-grained tasks, such as image processing, data transformation stages, or real-time analytics components.

A defining characteristic of serverless is the invocation model, where functions are triggered by events, either external or from other stages in a workflow. This event-driven approach lends itself to composability, allowing complex workflows to be constructed from loosely coupled function chains or directed acyclic graphs (DAGs). Orchestration platforms designed for serverless must address challenges associated with function cold starts, distributed state management, and end-to-end observability, as well as incorporate mechanisms for error handling and retries to maintain workflow resilience.

Edge computing complements serverless by relocating computation closer to data sources and end-users, thereby addressing latency, bandwidth, and autonomy constraints inherent in centralized cloud architectures. Workflows extended to the edge exploit geographically distributed nodes-ranging from local gateways to cellular base stations and micro data centers-to execute tasks with low latency and locality awareness. Orchestrating workflows across heterogeneous edge environments involves coordinating execution, managing intermittent connectivity, and adapting to variable resource capabilities. This adds complexity but yields significant benefits for latency-sensitive applications such as augmented reality, industrial automation, autonomous vehicles, and IoT analytics.

Edge orchestration frameworks adopt principles of decentralized control and fine-grained resource scheduling, often integrating with serverless runtimes optimized for constrained environments. Lightweight containerization and function-as-a-service (FaaS) models tailored for edge nodes facilitate rapid deployment and scaling under limited resource conditions. Moreover, advances in stateful function orchestration at the edge enable richer interactions and temporal computations, accommodating use cases that require continuous context awareness and data locality.

Adaptive scheduling strategies play a pivotal role in hybrid workflows combining cloud serverless platforms and edge nodes. Decisions about where to execute particular workflow stages hinge on latency requirements, data gravity, cost considerations, and fault tolerance constraints. Policies may dynamically migrate execution contexts based on real-time monitoring and predictive analytics, ensuring optimal resource utilization and service quality. For example, data preprocessing might be offloaded to edge locations to reduce upstream bandwidth, while computationally intensive training tasks are deferred to cloud serverless environments.

Programming models and APIs are evolving to abstract the complexity of this heterogeneity and to provide unified workflow descriptions capable of spanning serverless and edge domains. Frameworks leveraging domain-specific languages (DSLs) or extended DAG representations encapsulate deployment constraints, resource specifications, and data dependencies, thus enabling automated offloading and runtime optimization. The development of standardized interfaces and interoperable protocols facilitates federation among disparate orchestration engines and edge/cloud infrastructures.

Security and privacy considerations intensify in serverless and edge orchestration due to the distributed attack surface and multi-tenant environments. Workflow orchestration must integrate robust identity management, secure communication channels, and fine-grained access control policies. Edge computing scenarios further necessitate data encryption at rest and in transit, as well as trust mechanisms to validate execution integrity across diverse hardware and administrative domains.

Performance evaluation of serverless and edge orchestration systems incorporates metrics such as invocation latency, workflow completion time, throughput, resource utilization efficiency, and cost-effectiveness. Benchmarks are increasingly designed to mimic complex, multi-stage workflows with variable input rates and heterogeneous hardware profiles. Profiling tools and tracing frameworks provide insight into function execution patterns, aiding developers in tuning workflow components and deployment topologies.

The rise of serverless and edge computing introduces a new dimension to workflow orchestration by enabling event-driven, scalable workloads across distributed infrastructures that minimize infrastructure management overhead. The integration of these paradigms empowers systems to meet the demands of ultra-low-latency applications while fully leveraging decentralized resources. Continued advancements in orchestration abstractions, scheduling algorithms, and runtime support will be essential to unlocking the full potential of this promising execution landscape.

9.2. AI and Autonomous Workflow Management

The integration of artificial intelligence (AI) within workflow management systems represents a pivotal evolution in the orchestration of complex processes. Unlike traditional automation that follows rigid, predefined rules, AI-driven workflows exhibit adaptive, data-informed intelligence, enabling smarter orchestration that continuously evolves and optimizes itself. This section explores the mechanisms by which machine learning (ML) enhances workflow management, focusing on optimization opportunities, anomaly detection capabilities, and the development of self-healing, adaptive pipelines.

Fundamentally, AI enhances workflow management through the extraction and synthesis of insights from operational data streams. By continuously learning from historical and real-time performance metrics, ML models can predict bottlenecks, resource over-utilization, or failure points before they manifest explicitly. This predictive capability permits proactive adjustments to schedules, resource allocation, and execution strategies, effectively reducing downtime and improving throughput.

One of the primary AI-driven optimizations is intelligent scheduling. Traditional workflow systems often rely on static priority rules or heuristic algorithms that are ill-suited to the variability and scale of modern environments. In contrast, reinforcement learning (RL) techniques dynamically discover optimal scheduling policies by interacting with the system environment and receiving feedback in the form of resource usage efficiency or task completion times. Over time, RL agents refine their policies to maximize workflow performance metrics under changing conditions such as fluctuating workloads or variable hardware availability. This approach yields scheduling strategies resilient to complexity, surpassing manual configurations or standard optimization heuristics.

Another vital enhancement is AI-enabled anomaly detection within pipeline execution. Continuous monitoring of workflow tasks generates vast quantities of telemetry data, including execution durations, error rates, system logs, and resource consumption metrics. Machine learning algorithms, such as unsupervised clustering, autoencoders, or statistical models, establish baseline behavioral patterns. Deviations from these patterns, whether abrupt spikes in latency, unexpected error signatures, or resource exhaustion, are flagged automatically in real time. This proactive identification of anomalies accelerates fault localization and mitigates extended outages, enhancing the reliability and robustness of workflows.

Autonomous workflow management extends beyond anomaly detection when it incorporates self-healing capabilities. Upon detecting faults or suboptimal states, AI systems can initiate corrective actions without human intervention. Techniques such as causal inference help isolate root causes, while policy networks prescribe remediation steps-ranging from task retries, dynamic resource scaling, or fallback plan activations, up to partial rerouting within complex pipeline graphs. The integration of self-healing introduces resilience by enabling workflows to recover gracefully from unforeseen events, maintain SLAs (Service Level Agreements), and reduce operational overhead.

Adaptive pipelines forge an evolution where workflows are no longer static, linear sequences of tasks. Instead, they become fluid, intelligence-driven constructs that dynamically reconfigure their topology and parameters in response to shifting goals, input data characteristics, or environmental conditions. For example, AI models can detect when certain tasks become redundant due to changes in upstream data quality or suggest alternative processing paths that improve efficiency or accuracy. This adaptive orchestration relies heavily on continuous feedback loops and ML models capable of multi-objective optimization, balancing trade-offs such as speed, cost, and result fidelity.

The opportunities for AI-driven workflow management proliferate further with the convergence of advances in explainability and trustworthiness of ML models. Transparent decision-making processes enable operators to audit and validate AI recommendations, enhancing confidence in autonomous actions. Additionally, federated learning techniques allow distributed workflows to benefit collectively from shared intelligence while preserving data privacy and security constraints-particularly crucial in regulated environments or multi-tenant cloud architectures.

From an architectural perspective, implementing autonomous workflows entails embedding AI components at multiple levels: data ingestion, execution control, anomaly monitoring, and dynamic reconfiguration layers. This multi-tier integration demands careful orchestration of ML lifecycle management-encompassing model training, validation, deployment, and continuous updates-to maintain alignment with evolving workflows and business objectives. Moreover, scalability considerations mandate efficient data processing infrastructures and low-latency communication between AI services and workflow orchestration engines.

AI-powered autonomous workflow management marks a transformative shift from static automation to intelligent orchestration. The ability to optimize operations adaptively, detect and remedy anomalies proactively, and self-configure dynamically paves the way for highly resilient, efficient, and scalable process execution frameworks. Future workflows will increasingly resemble living systems-capable of learning from experience, anticipating challenges, and autonomously steering themselves toward optimal performance amidst complexity and change.

9.3. Cross-Platform Orchestration and Hybrid Cloud

The evolution of orchestration platforms reflects the increasing complexity and diversity of modern IT environments. Enterprises today require seamless integration across multiple cloud providers, private data centers, and edge infrastructures, collectively forming hybrid cloud architectures. Orchestration systems have emerged as the critical technology enabling unified control, deployment, and management of workloads spanning this heterogeneous ecosystem.

At its core, cross-platform orchestration addresses the fragmentation caused by disparate infrastructure abstractions, vendor-specific APIs, and varying operational models. Traditional cloud management tools, designed for isolated environments, cannot easily adapt to a hybrid reality where workloads dynamically migrate or interact across boundaries. This necessitates orchestration platforms that provide an abstraction layer decoupling workload definitions from underlying infrastructure specifics, thus enabling portability and interoperability.

A foundational architectural principle for hybrid cloud orchestration is the separation of concerns between declarative workflow specifications and platform-specific execution details. Declarative models describe what needs to be done-typically in the form of infrastructure as code (IaC), container orchestration manifests, or workflow graphs-while pluggable adapters translate these specifications into provider-native API calls and operational steps. Thus, orchestration engines function as meta-schedulers or controllers, managing lifecycle states and dependencies consistently across environments.

Among widely adopted orchestration frameworks, Kubernetes exemplifies this architectural approach by standardizing container orchestration across clouds and on-premises. However, pure Kubernetes deployments often require supplemental layers for multi-cloud or hybrid management scenarios. Tools such as Crossplane extend the Kubernetes control plane to provision and manage cloud resources uniformly via custom resource definitions (CRDs), allowing developers to declare cloud infrastructure in Kubernetes-native manifests. This bridges the operational gaps between cloud providers' proprietary services and on-premises deployments.

Another class of multi-platform orchestration frameworks leverages workflow engines that enforce portability through platform-agnostic execution models. Projects like Apache Airflow and Argo Workflows enable the definition of complex data and application pipelines decoupled from the underlying execution runtime. When integrated with infrastructure abstraction layers or multi-cloud resource managers, they achieve a level of interoperability where pipelines are orchestrated consistently, irrespective of underlying hardware or cloud vendor.

Architectural best practices for enabling true workflow portability include:

- **Infrastructure Abstraction:** Use declarative configuration languages (e.g., Terraform, Pulumi) or Kubernetes CRDs to represent infrastructure components consistently across clouds versus imperative scripts tied to specific APIs.

- **Modular Adapters and Connectors:** Design the orchestration engine with pluggable adapters that encapsulate provider-specific idiosyncrasies, allowing the main workflow logic to remain unchanged despite underlying platform differences.

- **State Management and Idempotency:** Maintain persistent, distributed state stores (e.g., etcd, Consul) in orchestration platforms to track resource states robustly, ensuring that re-executions or failovers yield consistent results, critical for hybrid environments with intermittent connectivity or heterogeneous SLAs.

- **Security and Compliance Uniformity:** Integrate policy engines such as Open Policy Agent (OPA) to enforce consistent access controls, configurations, and audit trails across all environments, reducing compromise risks due to platform-specific variations.

- **Event-Driven Integration:** Adopt event-driven architectures to connect disparate components and trigger cross-environment workflows with minimal latency, improving responsiveness and operational agility.

Consider a typical multi-cloud hybrid orchestration scenario involving an enterprise application decomposed into microservices and data processing workflows. The orchestration platform must deploy front-end and business logic components into a public cloud Kubernetes cluster for global availability, while sensitive data analytics processes execute on dedicated on-premises hardware to meet compliance requirements.

In this context, the orchestration platform:

- Defines the full application lifecycle as code, specifying deployment units, inter-service dependencies, and configuration parameters in a unified template.

- Utilizes provider-specific adapters to instantiate resources: provisioning managed Kubernetes clusters and cloud storage buckets in a public cloud, while integrating with local hypervisors and network services on-premises.

- Synchronizes state across distributed control planes, ensuring consistent versioning and rollback capabilities despite potential network partitions or cloud API rate limits.

- Coordinates cross-environment workflows, such as triggering secure data ingestion on-premises in response to cloud event notifications without manual intervention.

In practice, hybrid orchestration also demands robust tooling support for monitoring and diagnostics that span cloud and on-premises environments. Unified observability platforms aggregate logs, metrics, and traces regardless of origin, providing a holistic operational picture. This observability integration must align with the orchestration control plane for automated remediation and adaptive workload placement based on performance and cost metrics.

Emerging solutions like GitOps further enhance cross-platform workflow portability by coupling declarative infrastructure and application definitions with version-controlled repositories. Orchestration operators continuously reconcile desired states, irrespective of execution context, enabling consistent deployments and lifecycle management across hybrid environments.

The complexity of cross-platform orchestration frameworks inevitably introduces challenges, particularly in handling network heterogeneity, data gravity, and latency constraints. Consequently, architectural designs often embed configuration-driven policies to dynamically select optimal execution locations and scale resources in accordance with real-time telemetry, protecting workflow fidelity and responsiveness.

Cross-platform orchestration and hybrid cloud integrations rest upon unifying abstractions, modular extensibility, and declarative management. By adhering to these principles, organizations can transcend infrastructure silos and realize true workflow portability and interoperability, achieving operational continuity in a heterogeneous, multi-cloud world.

9.4. Community Ecosystem and Open Source Innovation

The Prefect ecosystem exemplifies the dynamic potential inherent in open source software development, propelled by a robust community and an agile culture of continuous innovation. The foundational architecture of Prefect was designed with extensibility and collaboration in mind, allowing developers and organizations to not only use the platform but also contribute meaningfully to its evolution. This section delves into how community engagement and open source practices have accelerated enhancements, diversified use cases, and ultimately shaped Prefect into a versatile orchestration framework for modern data workflows.

At the core of this ecosystem lies a vibrant developer community that spans individuals, enterprises, academic institutions, and cloud service providers. Contributors participate through multiple channels:

- Submitting code via pull requests,

- Reporting issues,

- Proposing feature enhancements,

- Authoring documentation,

- Sharing best practices via forums and social platforms.

This multi-faceted engagement ensures that the development process benefits from diverse perspectives and real-world domain expertise. For instance, contributions frequently originate from novel industry requirements or edge-case scenarios encountered by users in production environments, providing invaluable input that informs practical feature prioritization.

Prefect's open source repository on GitHub acts as a collaborative hub where transparent version control and peer review underpin a rigorous quality assurance process. Automated pipelines for continuous integration and testing enforce consistent code standards, while community-driven discussions in issues and pull requests facilitate peer validation and iterative refinement. This transparent and inclusive development lifecycle contrasts with monolithic or proprietary enterprise software models by fostering trust, rapid feedback, and shared ownership. The resultant rapid innovation cycle leads to frequent releases and incremental improvements that address both foundational system robustness and advanced workflow capabilities.

A notable aspect of community-driven innovation within Prefect is the expansion of workflows beyond the platform's original scope. Initially focused on providing reliability and observability for batch data pipeline orchestration, Prefect's capabilities have been extended by contributors to support:

- Event-driven architectures,

- Real-time data streams,

- Machine learning model training and deployment,

- Hybrid cloud scenarios.

These expanded use cases often emerge through contributions that integrate Prefect with other open source frameworks, such as Kubernetes, Apache Airflow, Spark, or distributed messaging systems. The modular design enables seamless adapters and custom task libraries to inhabit the ecosystem, augmenting Prefect's utility while maintaining the coherence of its core engine.

User feedback loops are deeply embedded in the ecosystem's operational model. Community forums, feature request boards, and frequent surveys collect insights into pain points and emergent needs. Project maintainers actively engage with users via live discussions and conference presentations, incorporating this intelligence into roadmap planning. This fluid exchange not only accelerates feature development but also ensures backward compatibility and stability, as maintainers weigh user impact carefully. Furthermore, the community's commitment to open standards and interoperability reduces vendor lock-in risks, enabling users to tailor Prefect deployments to their unique infrastructure and governance policies.

From a governance standpoint, Prefect has adopted a meritocratic model that balances contribution-driven influence with a stable core team providing strategic direction and release management. Contributors with sustained, high-quality input earn commit rights and decision-making roles, fostering a healthy incentive structure that encourages sustained involvement. This framework preserves agility while preventing fragmentation or dilution of project focus-a critical factor as the ecosystem grows in complexity and scale.

The open source foundation also drives innovation through ecosystem tools and extensions developed alongside the core platform. Community members have authored rich libraries of reusable tasks, credential managers, and monitoring integrations that extend Prefect's functional reach. Several community-driven projects implement domain-specific solutions, such as bioinformatics pipelines, financial data workflows, or real-time anomaly detection systems. These shared assets reduce duplication of effort and accelerate adoption across industries, reflecting the collective intelligence and specialization embedded in the community fabric.

The ongoing success and evolution of Prefect hinge on an intertwined cycle of open source collaboration, user-driven design, and rapid community innovation. The platform's adaptability and feature set continue to expand well beyond initial conceptions, driven by the contributions and feedback of a diverse and engaged group of practitioners. This community ecosystem is not merely an ancillary aspect but a core strategic asset, enabling Prefect to maintain technological leadership in workflow orchestration and to advance the state of the art through collective endeavor.

9.5. Evolving Standards and Interoperability

Orchestration platforms have undergone significant evolution, primarily driven by the increasing complexity of distributed workflows and the heterogeneity of the computing environments they span. This evolution hinges upon developing and adopting standards that promote interoperability, portability, and extensibility. Modern orchestration standards and protocols are foundational to enabling cross-platform compatibility and seamless data exchange, essential in multi-cloud, hybrid cloud, and on-premises deployments.

One of the critical advances in this domain is the maturation of workflow definition languages that standardize how workflows are described, abstracting the orchestration mechanisms away from any particular platform implementation. The Common Workflow Language (CWL) and Workflow Definition Language (WDL) have emerged as prominent open standards in scientific and data-intensive domains. They specify schemas for expressing tasks, dependencies, inputs, outputs, and metadata, enabling workflow portability and reproducibility across different engines and infrastructures. Both CWL and WDL emphasize declarative constructs for defining workflows as directed acyclic graphs (DAGs) of computational steps, which enhances the clarity and modularity of complex pipelines.

Beyond workflow definition languages, the development of standardized execution APIs further facilitates interoperability in orchestration ecosystems. Such APIs define uniform interfaces for workflow submission, status monitoring, execution control, and result retrieval, enabling clients and orchestrators to interact without tightly coupled implementations. The Open API Initiative and related efforts aim to formalize these protocols often through RESTful designs, supporting broad language and platform compatibility. Common APIs abstract vendor-specific orchestration details, lowering integration barriers and accelerating ecosystem growth. For example, the Workflow Execution Service (WES) specification, promulgated by the Global Alliance for Genomics and Health (GA4GH), establishes a protocol for launching and tracking workflows across heterogeneous backends, facilitating federated compute environments.

Prefect's architecture and design philosophy align closely with these emerging standards. By adopting universal concepts such as DAG-based workflow representations, clear state transitions, and modular task definitions, Prefect naturally integrates into the evolving interoperability landscape. Prefect supports serialization of scripted workflows into JSON and YAML formats that are readily transferable and interpretable by tooling built around standardized workflow definitions. This compatibility enables Prefect workflows to be shared or migrated with minimal friction, reinforcing reproducible analytics and collaborative development.

Moreover, Prefect actively contributes to and benefits from open-source ecosystems that drive standardization. Its open-core architecture and comprehensive API design resonate well with RESTful principles that underlie contemporary workflow execution specifications. Prefect's REST API exposes endpoints for flow registration, execution orchestration, state inspection, and event-driven triggers, embodying key functionalities envisaged by standardized execution APIs like WES. This alignment empowers developers and integrators to build tooling and user interfaces atop Prefect's execution layer without being constrained by proprietary communication protocols.

Prefect's integration strategies also embrace interoperability through extensibility mechanisms supporting a variety of compute environments and data exchange formats. By incorporating adapters and plugins for cloud-native platforms such as Kubernetes, Amazon Web Services, and Google Cloud Platform, Prefect workflows become portable across diverse infrastructures, leveraging native APIs while maintaining consistent orchestration semantics. Additionally, Prefect's data handling capabilities incorporate standardized serialization methods including Apache Arrow and Parquet for efficient, schema-aware data interchange, streamlining cross-tool compatibility.

Another key area where Prefect leverages evolving standards is event-driven workflow execution. Standards like CloudEvents define a common structure for describing event metadata that facilitates event notification and reaction across distributed systems. Prefect's support for event-based triggers, including sensors and callbacks, can be integrated within CloudEvents-driven architectures, enabling workflows to respond dynamically to external stimuli sourced from disparate platforms. This event interoperability propels Prefect toward seamless integration in complex orchestration scenarios such as hybrid cloud workflows and federated data environments.

Security and provenance considerations are becoming mandatory aspects of orchestration standards. Prefect benefits from and contributes to open standards around authentication, authorization, and audit logging within orchestration pipelines. By adopting OpenID Connect (OIDC) for identity federation and complying with OAuth 2.0 protocols, Prefect systems can participate securely in federated ecosystems. Additionally, Prefect's metadata tracking aligns with emerging standards for workflow provenance, ensuring that execution histories, input-output mappings, and versioned workflow artifacts are captured in machine-readable formats, crucial for compliance and reproducibility.

Interoperability is also fostered by the emergence of language-agnostic SDKs and adapters that encapsulate the complexity of underlying platforms. Prefect's Python-native SDK is complemented by community efforts aiming to provide interfaces in other popular languages, broadening its applicability across organizational tech stacks. This multi-language support streamlines integration with continuous integration/continuous deployment (CI/CD) pipelines, data engineering frameworks, and business intelligence tools, all of which benefit from consistent orchestration semantics enabled by standards alignment.

Finally, the open governance model surrounding Prefect encourages collaboration with standard development bodies and federated orchestration initiatives. This participatory approach facilitates early adoption and influence of new specifications, ensuring that Prefect remains at the forefront of interoperability trends. It also aids in harmonizing disparate technological ecosystems, which, without standardized protocols and definitions, risk fragmentation and increased operational complexity.

The landscape of orchestration standards and protocols continues to evolve rapidly, driven by the demands for interoperable and portable workflow automation. Prefect's alignment with these emerging norms-in workflow definitions, execution APIs, extensibility frameworks, security protocols, and event-driven paradigms-positions it as a pivotal contributor and beneficiary in the orchestration ecosystem. This synergy enhances Prefect's ability to operate across heterogeneous platforms and facilitates seamless data exchange, ultimately empowering sophisticated, scalable, and reproducible workflows in complex distributed environments.

9.6. Preparing for Next Generation Data Platforms

The evolution of data platforms is driven by the increasingly complex demands of real-time responsiveness, massive scale, and diverse data modalities. To remain effective, workflow orchestration frameworks must anticipate and adapt to these challenges by evolving beyond traditional batch processing paradigms toward architectures that seamlessly integrate streaming, real-time analytics, and distributed storage solutions.

A key consideration is the transition from monolithic data pipelines to microservices-based workflows that allow finer granularity in task execution, failure isolation, and resource allocation. Real-time analytics necessitates low-latency data processing, and orchestration frameworks must support event-driven architectures with dynamic scheduling capabilities to react immediately to trigger conditions or incoming data streams. This calls for the integration of message brokers, such as Apache Kafka or Pulsar, as first-class components within the orchestration fabric, ensuring reliable and ordered data delivery with backpressure mechanisms embedded at the workflow level.

Streaming architectures impose additional constraints on data consistency and state management. Therefore, workflows must evolve to handle continuous stateful computations, checkpointing, and time-window management effectively. Frameworks like Apache Flink or Spark Structured Streaming exemplify this paradigm, offering exactly-once processing semantics and robust fault-tolerance through distributed snapshots. Next-generation orchestration must incorporate these mechanisms natively or provide abstractions that simplify their configuration and monitoring. This integration enables developers to prototype hybrid workloads combining batch and streaming seamlessly, thus reducing operational complexity.

Distributed data lakes present another frontier requiring orchestration adaptation. These lakes span multiple clouds or on-premises environments and ingest unstructured, semi-structured, and structured data at massive scales. Coordination across heterogeneous storage technologies—ranging from object stores like Amazon S3 and Azure Data Lake Storage to distributed file systems such as HDFS—complicates metadata management, data governance, and pipeline versioning. Future-ready orchestration platforms will adopt unified metadata layers and schema registries, enabling lineage tracking, impact analysis, and fine-grained access control across disparate datasets. Emphasis on data format interoperability, such as Parquet, ORC, and Delta Lake, further reduces friction when constructing pipelines that interoperate across different processing engines.

Security and compliance considerations must be embedded within orchestration to address increasing regulatory scrutiny and data privacy concerns. Role-based access control (RBAC), encryption key management, and audit logging need to interface tightly with workflow triggers, ensuring that sensitive operations undergo appropriate review and that data movement conforms to policy constraints. The orchestration platform itself will require enhanced observability with support for distributed tracing and anomaly detection powered by machine learning, enabling rapid diagnosis of failures or performance degradation in complex multi-component pipelines.

Automation powered by declarative infrastructure as code (IaC) will facilitate reproducible, consistent deployment of end-to-end workflows across development, testing, and production environments. Integrating orchestration with container orchestration platforms such as Kubernetes enables portability, scalability, and resource isolation necessary to run heterogeneous workloads. Scheduling policies will increasingly leverage workload characteristics and data locality heuristics to optimize resource utilization and minimize data movement overhead.

Finally, next-generation orchestration frameworks will embrace extensibility and interoperability standards to accommodate emerging technologies and heterogeneous ecosystems. Plugin architectures allowing custom connectors, task types, and user-defined operators will empower data engineers and scientists to tailor workflows to domain-specific requirements. Open standards for workflow definitions, such as the Common Workflow Language (CWL) or Workflow Description Language (WDL), will promote portability and ease integration with analytics, machine learning, and visualization tools.

In preparation for next-generation data platforms, orchestration must embrace real-time event-driven models, stateful streaming computations, distributed metadata management, stringent security, and cloud-native automation. These adaptations will collectively enable the management of complex, scalable, and compliant data pipelines, positioning organizations to harness the full potential of tomorrow's data infrastructure.